Hybrid Financial Instruments

HYBRID FINANCIAL INSTRUMENTS

Brian Coyle

FINANCIAL WORLD Publishing
THE CHARTERED INSTITUTE OF BANKERS

Financial World Publishing
IFS House
4-9 Burgate Lane
Canterbury
Kent
CT1 2XJ
United Kingdom

Telephone: 01227 818687

Financial World Publishing publications are published by
The Chartered Institute of Bankers, a non-profit-making registered educational charity.

Typeset by Kevin O'Connor
Printed in Italy

ISBN 0-85297-457-4

Contents

1

What are Hybrids?

The term hybrid means something composed of two or more widely differing elements. A hybrid financial instrument is a security containing two elements, equity and debt, that could be described as either a bond with equity features or a share with debt characteristics. The term may be used more loosely when referring to any financial instrument that combines features of two or more financial instruments.

Although they are not used as extensively as straight equity or debt securities in the capital markets, hybrid securities may serve the dual function of:

- providing companies with a means of raising capital at a reasonable cost, and
- providing investors with an attractive method of investment as an alternative or supplement to debt and equity in their investment portfolio.

The popularity of hybrids among investors and issuers (companies) varies with conditions in the capital markets. Equity-linked bonds can be attractive to some investors when share prices are volatile or uncertain because they offer the comfort of some interest income with the chance to benefit from an upturn in share prices.

Characteristics of Debt and Equity

A company's debt capital such as bonds, is borrowed money. The company has financial obligations to its lenders:

- to repay borrowed capital, perhaps at a premium, at some time in the future and/or
- to pay interest on borrowed capital.

Straight debt requires interest to be payable on borrowed capital until maturity, when the debt principal is finally repaid. There are some exceptions, namely:

- perpetual debt or undated loan stock: the borrower not being obliged to repay the debt principal at all, but to continue to pay interest on the debt in perpetuity
- zero-coupon bonds and discount paper: the borrower does not pay interest, but undertakes to pay a specified amount of principal at maturity. The investor makes a return by purchasing the debt at below its face value, and making a gain from the difference between the discounted purchase price and the eventual redemption value.

A company's equity is its owners' capital. Equity shareholders have the right to participate in the profits of a company to an unlimited extent, in proportion to the number of shares they hold, but only after the company has settled its obligations to other providers of capital, such as holders of debt securities. They are the ultimate owners of a company, sharing whatever residual profits there may be after the payments of interest and dividends to other capital providers who have a prior right to payment. If the company is dissolved and its affairs wound up, equity shareholders would be entitled to the net proceeds from selling off the company's assets, but only after all prior rights to payment have been settled.

Equity capital is created in several ways:

- by issuing new shares for cash
- by issuing new shares for other assets, such as in exchange for the shares of a newly acquired subsidiary
- by retaining profits within the company and building up shareholders' reserves

Relative Risk of Debt and Equity

There are financial risks for investors in both debt and equity capital. These are largely price risk and, in the case of bonds, credit risk.

Bondholders have to take into account

- the credit risk that the company will fail to pay interest or repay the debt principal in full and on schedule, and
- the risk of a fall in the market value of their bonds.

The financial risks for equity shareholders, however, are higher. The annual income from their shares is uncertain, depending on company profits. They share in profits only after the company's obligations to other providers of capital have been settled. Before equity dividends can be paid, interest must be paid on debt capital, and dividends must be paid to non-equity shareholders. Equity shareholders also must share in any losses the company makes.

The value of equity shares can be volatile, share prices can fall sharply when prospects for profits and dividends take a turn for the worse. Because a company's profits can fluctuate from one year to the next, or go through business cycles of growth and decline, the annual profit per share and the annual dividend per share are uncertain. The risk must always exist that the returns to equity shareholders will be less than anticipated, possibly less than in the previous year and even negative. This risk explains the greater volatility of equity share prices compared with bond prices.

In spite of the risks, both debt and equity capital have attractive features for investors. Debt capital can provide a predictable stream of future income and can be regarded as a low-risk investment. This may be contrasted with equity capital that can provide its owners with rising annual income when the company is successful, and the chance to make money out of their company's success.

Hybrid instruments contain elements of debt and equity. They have some of the lower-risk defensive qualities of debt capital, offering investors the security of regular interest income and the prospect of repayment at maturity. At the same time, they give their holders the opportunity to obtain an equity stake in the company and share in its profits if the company should be successful.

Types of Hybrid Instrument

Hybrid instruments might be classified as either equity or debt. In the balance sheet of a company, hybrids might be shown as equity or debt, or perhaps as a mixture of the two. For measuring the net worth of a borrower, a loan covenant might include a hybrid instrument as part of the borrower's net worth, or might exclude it, depending on the preferred definition of net worth.

The financial reporting of hybrids is described briefly in Chapter 10.

The hybrid instruments described in this book are:

- equity-linked bonds and
- preferred stock, or preference shares.

Equity-linked Bonds

Equity-linked debt securities give their holder the right at some time in the future to subscribe for equity. They include:

- convertible bonds (convertibles). These give the holder the right at some date in the future to exchange their bonds into new equity shares of the bond issuer, at a specified rate of conversion
- exchangeable bonds (exchangeables). These give the holder the right at some date in the future to exchange their bonds into existing equity shares of a company other than the bond issuer, at a specified rate of conversion
- bonds with share warrants attached (equity warrant bonds). The share warrants can be used at some date in the future to subscribe for new shares in the company at a specified price.

It is generally expected that between the date of issuing equity-linked securities and the time that the security holders are allowed to take up equity shares, the share price will have risen. This assumption is built into the rate for the conversion of debt into equity or the subscription price for warrants.

Preferred Stock (Preference Shares)

Preferred stock (preference shares) are non-equity shares. Some preferred stock has characteristics similar to debt capital, including an option to convert into equity, and can be regarded as a form of hybrid.

This book describes these main types of hybrid instrument, including their structure, purpose and valuation, and the capital markets for hybrid instruments.

Convertible Bonds and Exchangeable Bonds

This chapter explains the features of convertible bonds, or convertibles, and another type of equity-linked bond, exchangeable bonds. Exchangeable bonds are similar in many respects to convertibles, and so most of this chapter focuses on convertibles.

Convertible Bonds (Convertibles)

Convertible bonds, also known as convertible debentures and convertible loan stock, are unsecured fixed-interest bonds. They give their holder the right, but not the obligation, to convert the bonds into equity shares of the issuing company, but only under specified terms and conditions. If the bonds are not converted into equity, they must be redeemed at or before maturity by the issuer.

Coupon

Convertibles have a fixed-coupon rate of interest. The coupon rate is lower than the coupon that would have to be paid on straight debt issued at the same time and for the same maturity. The lower coupon reflects the benefit to the bondholder of the option to convert into equity. For example, a company might be able to issue five-year convertible bonds at a coupon of 4.5% when the coupon on straight five-year bonds might be 6.5%. The coupon payable on a convertible bond depends not on market rates of interest at the time of issue only, but also on the terms and conditions of the issue, such as whether there is a put option for bondholders. (Put options are described later.) Interest, that is payable so long as the convertibles remain in the form of bonds, usually is paid every six months, but payments can be made annually.

Redemption

Convertible bonds, if not converted into equity shares by their holder, are redeemed at maturity or earlier by the issuer. Each issue of convertible bonds has a redemption date, the date by which the issuer must redeem the bonds if they have not been converted into equity shares. Usually bonds are redeemable at par on this date.

The final redemption date could be from five years to 30 years from the date of issue. In practise convertibles are either converted into equity or redeemed before maturity, because:

- the final conversion date is earlier than the maturity of the bond, or
- early redemption (or conversion) is enforced through the exercise of call or put options.

An issue of convertible bonds might include an *event-risk clause* in its terms and conditions. This gives the bondholders the right to demand immediate redemption of the bonds in the event of the issuer merging with or being taken over by another company.

Rights to Payment

While convertible bonds remain in bond form – until they are converted into equity – the bondholders have various rights that are set out in the terms and conditions of the issue. These include:

- a right to prompt payment of interest on specified dates and
- prompt payment on redemption, should the bonds be redeemed rather than converted.

A failure by the issuer to pay promptly or in full would be an event of default, giving the bondholders the right to demand accelerated repayment of the debt principal.

In the event of liquidation of the issuer's business, convertible bondholders would rank as unsecured creditors behind secured creditors but ahead of equity investors in the right to payment from the proceeds of selling off the company's assets.

Covenants

Convertible bonds are issued with covenants attached with which the issuer undertakes to comply with certain conditions, until the bonds are converted or redeemed.

In jurisdictions that provide for trusts, notably the US and UK, there may be a trust deed for a bond issue. The trustees, usually a specialist corporation, act in the interests of the bondholders who are the beneficiaries under the trust, and in accordance with the terms of the trust deed. The trust deed will include the covenants protecting the bondholders.

Parent Company Guarantee

An issue of either straight bonds or convertible bonds by a subsidiary company within a group usually is guaranteed by the parent company. It is quite common for bonds to be issued by a special-purpose subsidiary which is required to raise finance in its own name, but on behalf of operational companies in the group. For example, some multinational groups have established special finance subsidiaries in the Netherlands, whose function is to raise debt finance for the group. Bonds issued by a finance subsidiary give the right to convert into equity shares of the parent company.

The guarantee of the parent company adds the credit standing of the parent and the group as a whole, to the bond. Without the parent-company guarantee, bonds issued by a subsidiary might be given a junk bond credit rating, making the bonds difficult to issue to investors except at a high rate of interest or very favorable rates of conversion into equity.

Conversion Rights

Convertible bondholders have the right to convert their bonds into equity shares under specified terms and conditions.

The right to convert must be exercised on:

- a specified conversion date, or
- on any of several conversion dates, typically a specified date each year over a period of several years, or
- during a conversion period, at any time between two specified dates.

For example, an issue of convertible bonds could allow bondholders to exercise the right to convert into equity on September 1 during each of the years 2004-2008. A convertible bond might even give the right of conversion into equity *at any time* from the issue date for the bond up to its maturity.

Conversion Ratio

Bonds are convertible into a specified number of equity shares. The conversion ratio is the number of shares into which a bond can be converted. When bondholders can convert bonds into equity in each of a number of consecutive years, the conversion ratio usually is different for each year.

A conversion ratio is expressed as the number of shares that can be obtained by converting bonds with a face value of 1,000, $1,000 or $1,000, depending on the currency of the bond.

Example
A company issued 5.5% Guaranteed Convertible Capital Bonds 2012 with a conversion ratio of 384.62 for each $1,000 bond. Each bond can be converted into 384.62 shares.

Conversion Price
The conversion price is the share price at which a bond can be converted into equity. It is established when an issue of convertible bonds is made. The conversion price invariably is higher than the current equity share price at the time of the bond issue. In effect, it is the minimum market price that the shares must reach before the bondholders will want to exercise their right to convert their bonds into equity.

The conversion price is calculated as follows:

$$\text{Conversion price} = \frac{\text{Redemption value of bond*}}{\text{Conversion ratio}}$$

Note
The redemption value of the bond at maturity is used in the calculation of the conversion price and normally is par value, unless the bondholders have a put option. Put options are described later.

Example
A company issues 5.5% convertible bonds at par. The conversion ratio is 384.62 shares for every $1,000 of bonds.

This means the conversion price is $1,000/384.62 = 260¢. When the bonds are first issued, the company's current share price will be below 260¢.

The conversion price for an issue most often is established before the conversion ratio. The conversion ratio being calculated from the conversion price, rather than the other way round.

There is an inverse relationship between the conversion price and the conversion ratio. A higher conversion price means a lower conversion ratio. A reduction in the conversion price would mean a higher conversion ratio.

Exercise
Attempt your own solution to the following problem.

A company raised $128 million before deducting issue costs, from an issue at par of a 15-year 5.25% euroconvertible bond. The bonds have a conversion price of $25.80 compared with a price of $21.70 at the end of the day the bond issue was made. What is the conversion ratio, and how many new shares will be created if all bondholders exercise their conversion rights?

Solution
Conversion ratio per $1,000 of bonds = $1,000 ÷ $25.80 per share

= 38.7597 shares per $1,000 bonds

$$\text{Number of new shares} = \frac{\text{Proceeds from issue (before deducting issue costs)}}{\text{Conversion price}}$$

$$= \frac{\$128 \text{ million}}{\$25.80}$$

$$= 4{,}961{,}240 \text{ shares}$$

Conversion Premium

When convertibles are issued, the conversion price is higher than the current market value of the shares into which they can be converted. The difference between the price of the convertible bonds and the market value of the shares into which they can be converted is called the conversion premium. In most cases this premium is measured as a percentage of the current market value of the shares into which the bonds can be converted.

Example
A company issues convertible bonds at par, giving their holders the right to convert their bonds into shares in five years' time. The conversion ratio is 228.5714 shares for each $1,000, face value, of bonds. At the time of the issue, the shares had a market price of $3.50 each.

Analysis
At the time of issuing the bonds, each $1,000 of bonds at the issue price, carry the right to convert into shares currently worth $800 (228.5714 x $3.50).

	$
Issue price (= current price of bonds)	1,000
Value of shares	800
Conversion premium	200

The conversion premium is 25% (200 ÷ 800 x 100%) of the current value of the shares into which the bonds can be converted.

Another way of making the calculation is as follows:

	$
Conversion price (1,000 ÷ 228.5714)	4.375
Current share price	3.500
Conversion premium	0.875

The conversion premium is (0.875/3.50) x 100% = 25%.

Parity Value (Conversion Value)
The current market value of the shares into which a bond can be converted is its parity value or conversion value.

Parity Value = (number of shares into which a bond can be converted) x (current price per share).

A conversion premium can be shown by the formula

$$\frac{\text{Current price of bond} - \text{Parity value}}{\text{Parity value}} \times 100\%$$

Example

A convertible bond carries the right of conversion into 360 shares per $1,000 bonds. The current share price is 275¢ and the current price of the convertible is 115.

Analysis

The parity value is $990 (360 x 275¢) per $1,000 of bonds.

The conversion premium is currently $\frac{1150 - 990}{990} \times 100\% = 16.2\%$.

Size of the Conversion Premium when Bonds are Issued

The size of a conversion premium when a convertible is issued might be in the region of 15% to 25%. It will be affected by a number of factors, including the following:

- The coupon rate of interest payable on the bond. The closer the coupon rate is to the rate payable on a straight bond, the higher the premium will be. A lower premium would be needed to compensate investors in convertible bonds for a low coupon rate compared to straight bonds.
- Expectations about the future rate of increase in the share price of the issuer. A higher conversion premium can be obtained when the share price is expected to rise strongly in the future.
- Current conditions in the convertible bond market.

Changes Over Time in the Conversion Premium

The conversion premium changes over time, with changes in the market price of

- the convertible bond itself, and

- the shares into which the bond can be converted

Over time, the share price will change. One of the attractions of convertible bonds to investors is the prospect that the share price will increase and eventually exceed the conversion price. When the share price rises, the size of the conversion premium should fall in size, although the market price of the convertible also will rise as the share price goes up.

Example
A company has issued convertible bonds with a conversion ratio of 228.5714 shares per $1,000 of bonds, and a conversion price of $4.375. Suppose that two years later, the share price of the company has risen to $4.20, and the market price of the convertibles has risen to 104. The conversion premium now would be much smaller, as follows:

	$
Current market price of convertible bonds	1,040
Current market price of equivalent shares (228.5714 x $4.20)	960
Conversion premium	80

The conversion premium is now 8.33% (80 ÷ 960 x 100%). It has fallen, in spite of a rise in the market price of the bonds, because the market value of the shares has gone up.

Conversion Discount

A conversion discount is a negative conversion premium.

Example
A convertible bond has a current market price of 98. The conversion price is $2.50 per share. The current share price is $2.60.

Analysis
Each $1,000 of bonds (nominal value) can be converted into 400 shares

($1,000 ÷ $2.50 per share). The parity value, the current market value of the shares into which the bonds can be converted, is $1,040 for each $1,000 bonds at nominal value (400 shares x $26).

The conversion premium is negative because the price of the convertible is only 98 (or $980 per $1,000 of bonds).

	$
Market price of convertible	980
Current parity value	1,040
Conversion discount	60

This can be expressed as 5.77% of the parity value (60 ÷ 1,040 x 100%).

How Can a Conversion Discount Arise?
A conversion discount will occur only in unusual circumstances. This is because, as the issuer's share price rises above the conversion price, the market price of the convertible will rise also, reflecting the increasing value of the conversion rights on the bond. A conversion discount should occur only when:

- the share price is abnormally and temporarily high, or when
- the market price of the convertible is abnormally and temporarily low.

A share's price could be abnormally high during a period of speculation about a takeover bid. A convertible's secondary-market price could be low when there is very weak demand in the market to buy convertibles, that is the market could be temporarily thin.

Changing the Conversion Price

The terms and conditions of a convertible bond issue should provide for a change in the conversion price when the issuer does something after the bonds have been issued to affect the market value of its shares. Typically, the issuer may take a course of action that results in a lower share price. A fall in the share price will increase the conversion premium and reduce the market value of the convertible bonds. To compensate the bondholders, the company should reduce the conversion price and so increase the number of shares that can be obtained by converting the bonds, i.e. increase the conversion ratio.

The conversion price might be reduced and the conversion ratio increased if the company takes any specified action or if any other event occurs with the issuer's consent that will dilute or reduce the value of its equity shares. These actions include:

- making a bonus issue (scrip issue) of shares
- selling off a major subsidiary in the group
- paying an abnormally high dividend to shareholders.

Example
A company has issued convertible bonds with a conversion ratio of 400 shares for each $1,000 of bonds, and a conversion price of 250¢. The current share price of the company is 220¢, that makes the conversion premium about 13.6%.

Suppose that the company now sells one of its major operating subsidiaries, and distributes the profits from the sale to its shareholders, in the form of a special dividend. As a result of the sell-off and dividend payment, the share price after the dividend payment falls by about 20%, from 220¢ to 176¢. The terms of the bond issue should require the trustees for the bondholders to agree a reduction in the conversion price with the company. In this example, the conversion price might be reduced by 20%, from 250¢ to 200¢, or even less.

Another situation in which a reduction in the conversion price would be required would follow a bonus issue of shares by the company. A bonus issue, also known as a capitalization issue or scrip issue, involves an issue of new shares, at no cost, to existing shareholders in proportion to their current shareholding. The inevitable consequence of a bonus issue will be a fall in the market price of the issuer's shares.

Suppose for example that a company that has issued convertible bonds makes a 1 for 2 bonus issue of shares. As a result, existing shareholders receive, free of charge, one new share for every two shares they hold. The number of shares in issue will rise by 50%, and the share price is likely to fall correspondingly, by about one third. To protect the interests of the convertible bondholders, the conversion ratio for the bonds should be increased by 50%. This would mean a reduction in the conversion price by one third.

Call Option

A call option on a convertible bond gives the issuer the right to redeem the bonds before final maturity at a predetermined price at any time during a call period. The call period typically begins a few years after the bonds have been issued and continues up to maturity. It could, however, begin immediately, from the time of the issue.

Once a call option has been exercised, holders of the convertible bonds usually have a short time during which they can exercise their right to convert the bonds into equity. Bonds that are not converted are then redeemed.

Call Option

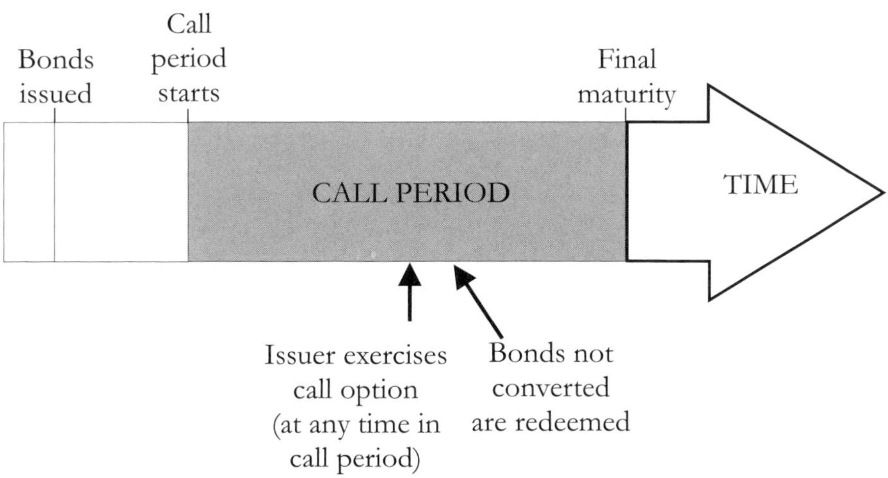

The right to exercise the call option could be dependent on the issuer's share price having reached a specified trigger level (a provisional call). An issue of convertibles could, however, give the issuer an absolute right of call, without pre-conditions, during the call period.

Example 1

A company issues a convertible bond with a conversion price of $4. The conversion premium on issue is 25%. The bond is callable five years after the issue date at 102, six years after the issue date at 101 and seven years after the issue date at 100 (par value). However, the bond is callable between the end of year 5 and the end of year 7 only if the share price has increased to 140% of the conversion price - i.e. to $5.60 or higher.

Analysis

The company has a call option, but can exercise it and force bondholders to convert into equity or redeem the bonds, only from the end of year 5 onwards. For the next two years, until the end of year 7, the right to call is provisional on the share price having risen by 40% since the bonds were issued. At this share price, it would be more profitable for bondholders to convert into equity, if a call were made, than to let the company redeem the bonds at 102, 101 or 100.

Example 2

A convertible bond issue in the euroconvertible bond market gives bondholders the right to convert their bonds into ordinary shares at a conversion price of 318¢. The company has call options to redeem the bonds before maturity, or force bondholders to convert into equity, but only if the share price exceeds a stated percentage of the conversion price. This percentage rose over time, as follows:

	Share price must exceed:	
	% of conversion price	**Share price in cents**
Before May 21 Year 5	135	429.3
From May 21 Year 5 to May 20 Year 6	137	435.7
From May 21 Year 6 to May 20 Year 7	143	454.7
From May 21 Year 7 to May 20 Year 8	150	477.0
From May 21 Year 8 to May 20 Year 9	157	499.3
From May 21 Year 9 to May 20 Year 10	165	524.7

There are two main circumstances under which an issuer could exercise a call option.

- Other convertible bondholders could have already exercised their right to convert their bonds into shares. Exercising the call option would be intended to force the remaining bondholders to convert.
- Fixed interest rates on bonds could have fallen since the convertibles were issued.

The coupon rate on convertibles is lower than the coupon rate on straight debt. However, a large fall in the general level of interest rates on bonds could prompt an issuer of convertibles to redeem the bonds and possibly seek refinance by issuing new bonds at a lower coupon. For example, if convertibles were issued with a coupon of 7% and a call option, the coupon that would have to be charged on straight bonds with the same maturity might be 9%. If the general level of interest rates falls, the bond issuer might exercise the call option and redeem the bonds, and finance the cost of redeeming the bonds by making a new issue of either straight bonds, at 6.5% for example, or convertibles at an even lower interest rate.

Put Option

Some issues of convertible bonds include a put option. This gives the bondholders the right to demand early redemption of the bonds, before the final maturity date. Early redemption might be at par, but is more usually at a premium to par.

The put option typically is exercisable at any time from a specified date several years after the bonds are issued, up to final maturity.

Put options could present a danger if the company were forced to seek refinancing to redeem the bonds, and holders chose to exercise their put option. In many cases, the company could raise new capital to redeem its bonds, but its ability to do so will depend on its financial situation. If a company is in financial difficulties, it might be unable to borrow further to refinance its requirements, i.e. to redeem the convertibles at the put-option date.

Types of Convertible Bond

Convertible bonds can be classified into five broad types:

- conventional convertibles
- low-premium convertibles
- discount convertibles
- rolling-premium put convertibles
- single-premium put convertibles
- liquid-yield option notes (zero-coupon convertibles)

Conventional Convertibles

A conventional convertible is a bond whose conversion premium on issue is considered normal or usual by the market. The conversion premium on issue typically is between 15% and 25%.

The coupon rate of interest is lower than the coupon on straight fixed-rate debt with the same maturity. The minimum saving on the coupon for convertible bonds compared with the coupon for straight fixed-rate bonds is at least 50 basis points (0.50%), but often is more. When the conversion premium is high, investors have to be compensated with a high coupon yield.

Conventional convertibles can have a call option, but do not give bondholders a put option. Most convertibles issued in domestic bond markets, excluding Japan, and many euroconvertible issues, are of this conventional type.

Example
A convertible has a current conversion premium of 30% and five years to conversion date. It is offering a redemption yield to investors of 40 basis points (0.40%) above the yield available from investing in government bonds.

Analysis
The premium is on the high side of normal at 30%. However, the yield to bondholders is very low, just 40 basis points above the yield on risk-free government bonds. This indicates an excessive market price for the convertibles. Investors might be advised at this yield and price to sell the convertible and buy shares if they wished to have an equity involvement in the company.

At the time of issue, it is expected that conventional convertibles eventually will be converted into equity. This is because the average annual rise in the share price over the period to conversion date does not have to be large to make conversion worthwhile.

Example
A company issued $50 million of convertible bonds at par, for redemption after 15 years. The conversion price was $20. The conversion ratio therefore was 50 per $1,000 of bonds and the conversion premium on issue was 25%. The bonds can be converted at this rate from the end of year 10 onwards.

Analysis
The conversion premium on issue is the difference between the price of the convertible and the parity value, expressed as a proportion of the

parity value. Because the conversion premium is 25% of the parity value, it is 20% of the convertible's price. This can be shown for each $1,000 of bonds as follows:

	$
Price of the convertible (issued at par)	1,000
Parity value	800
Conversion premium (25% of parity value)	200

Because parity value is the number of shares into which the bonds can be converted (50 shares) multiplied by the current share price, the current share price must be $16 ($800 ÷ 50 shares).

The conversion price is $20 and the current share price $16. To make conversion worthwhile by the end of year 10, the share price must grow by at least $4 (25%) from the issue date. This means the average annual growth rate in the share price must be at least 2.25% ($\sqrt[10]{1.25} - 1$).

An annual growth in share price of 2.25% would be regarded as a modest target, and it should be expected that the bonds will be converted at the end of year 10.

Low-Premium Convertibles

Low-premium convertibles have a low conversion premium on issue. The probability that the bonds will be converted into equity is very high, because only a low average annual growth rate in share price is needed to make conversion worthwhile. And because the conversion premium is low, these bonds offer an even lower coupon than conventional convertibles.

Discount Convertibles

A discount convertible is a conventional convertible issued at a price below par, i.e. at a discount to par. The coupon is lower but the conversion premium is higher than for a conventional convertible bond. For example, a company that could issue a conventional ten-year convertible bond at par with a coupon of 6% and a conversion premium of 15%, might be able to issue a ten-year discount convertible at a price of 82.0, a coupon of just 4% but a conversion premium of 20%.

Rolling-Premium Put Convertibles

A premium put option is an option for the bondholder to demand redemption of the bond at a premium to par value. A rolling put is a series of two or more put options, at dates spread over a period of time.

A rolling-premium put convertible gives its holder a series of put options to redeem the bond before maturity at a premium to par value, at several dates up to maturity. The redemption price increases at each successive option exercise date. The coupon is lower than for conventional convertibles.

Rolling-premium put convertibles were first issued in the euroconvertibles market in Europe in 1988. They came into favor after the worldwide stock-market crash of October 1987. Companies and investors became aware that share prices can go down substantially and do not necessarily rise continually over time. When share prices fall, or even if share prices do not rise, there is a strong probability that convertible bonds with a put option will be redeemed early, with bondholders exercising their put option as soon as possible. To encourage bondholders to hold on to their bonds, and not redeem them at the earliest time possible, a rolling put-option convertible provides for a higher put price, i.e. a higher redemption price for the bonds, at each successive exercise date for the options. The rising redemption price will make it less likely that bondholders will exercise their right to redeem the bonds as soon as possible. Instead, they might hold onto the bonds to benefit from the rise in the redemption price at each successive option exercise date. At the same time, it becomes much less likely that the bonds will be converted into equity shares because the share price will have to rise by a large amount to make conversion a preferable choice for bondholders instead of redemption.

Example
A company issues ten-year convertible bonds on March 22 Year 1, offering a coupon of 5% and rolling put options. The rolling put options give bondholders the right to redeem their bonds as follows:

Option exercise date	Put price for redemption
At March 22 Year 6	121.156
At March 22 Year 7	126.666
At March 22 Year 8	132.699
At March 22 Year 9	139.306
At March 22 Year 10	146.540
At March 22 Year 11	154.461

In this example, put options are exercisable annually. For some convertible issues put options are exercisable less frequently. A bond issue with 15 years to maturity on issue could give bondholders the right to exercise a put option after five years at one price and after ten years at a higher price. There would be just two dates for exercising the option.

Single-Premium Put Convertibles

A single-premium put convertible is similar to a rolling-premium put convertible except that:

- there is only one opportunity to exercise the put option, i.e. just one put-option date
- the coupon is lower than for a rolling-premium put option, but the put price at which the bonds can be redeemed, in other words the yield to put, is higher.

The high price for redeeming the bonds increases the probability that the option will be exercised and so reduces the probability that the bonds will be converted into equity.

Example

Epsilon issued at par a single-premium put 15-year convertible bond in Year 1. The coupon yield was 4%. The terms of conversion are 600 shares in Epsilon for every $1,000 (face value) of bonds. The price of the share at the issue date was $1.40.

The bond has a put and a call option.

- The put option gives bondholders the right to redeem their bonds at 123.5 after five years from the issue date.
- The call option is exercisable at 103 one year after the issue date, and the redemption price then declines gradually each year. However, the bonds are not callable in the first five years unless the share price has risen to 130% or more of its initial conversion price.

Analysis

The convertible is unlikely to remain in issue beyond the put date. The bondholders have a choice after five years. They can either:

- redeem the bonds at 123.5, or
- hold onto the bonds, expecting to convert them into equity in the future at the rate of 600 shares per $1,000 of bonds.

The share price at the time of the bond issue was $1.40. At the put date at the end of the fifth year, bonds can be redeemed at a price of 123.5, giving an equivalent value of $2.06 per share ($1,235 ÷ 600 shares).

The decision to redeem at the put-option exercise date probably will be a now-or-never choice. If the bondholders decide to retain their bonds, the company almost certainly will exercise its call option very soon afterwards. Because the redemption price for the bonds is well below the put-option redemption price, the bondholders should either:

- wait for the call option and convert their bonds into equity, or
- redeem the bonds on the put date at the put-option price.

Bondholders would have to be confident, at the option exercise date at the end of the fifth year, that the share price will rise very soon to $2.06

or more. Otherwise they will exercise the put option to redeem the bonds. They would then be able to purchase shares, should they wish, in the stock market.

Liquid-Yield Option Notes

These are bonds that pay no interest, and are redeemable at maturity at par, unless they are converted into equity on or before maturity.

The terms of conversion are such that the share price must grow at a fairly high average annual rate to make conversion into equity worthwhile.

The probability that the notes will be redeemed, rather than converted into equity, is quite high, and the maturity (redemption) yield on these notes must be quite high to attract investors.

Example
Beta Inc issued $100 million of liquid-yield option notes. The initial conversion premium was 20%, and the share price at the time of issue was $50. The maturity of the notes was 15 years, and the issue was priced at 36.25 to give noteholders a yield of 7% per annum to maturity. ($36.25 \times 1.07^{15} = 100$.)

The notes have a put option, giving holders the right to redeem their notes at 50.84 five years from the issue date. This gives the same annual yield of 7% to the put option date on the issue price ($36.25 \times 1.07^{5} = 50.84$).

Analysis
The share price at the time of the issue of the notes was $50, and the conversion premium was 20%. The conversion price therefore was $60 ($50 x 1.20).

The conversion ratio is as follows:

$$\frac{\text{Initial price per \$1,000 note}}{\text{Conversion price}} = \frac{\$362.50}{\$60 \text{ per share}} = 6.042 \text{ shares}$$

At the put date five years later, the noteholders will have the choice of either:

- redeeming the notes at 50.84, i.e. at $508.40 for each $1,000 (nominal value) of notes, or
- retaining their notes with the right to convert into 6.042 shares.

The value to noteholders of the put option can be expressed as a value per equivalent share. This is the amount the noteholders would receive on redemption of the notes for giving up the right to convert into equity. In this example, the value of the put option per share would be $84.14 ($508.40 ÷ 6.042 shares). This represents an increase in the share price, above its price at the time of the issue, of $34.14 ($84.14 – $50 per share). In other words, unless the share price rises by over 68% between the issue of the notes and the put option exercise date five years later, noteholders could be tempted to exercise their put option.

For conversion to be worthwhile at a future date, a large annual growth in share price will be essential. There is a strong probability that the put option will be exercised after five years.

Zero-coupon convertible bonds

In the UK, liquid-yield option notes are known as zero-coupon convertible bonds.

The features of each type of convertible bond are summarized in the table on the next page.

Summary

Types of Convertible

	Conventional	Low premium	Rolling premium put	Single premium put	Liquid-yield option notes
Coupon rate	Lower than on fixed-rate bonds with the same maturity	Lower than for conventional convertibles	Lower than for conventional convertibles	Lower than for rolling-premium put convertibles	Zero
Conversion premium on issue	Typically 10-30%	Typically about 5%	Typically 10-30%	Typically 10-30%	Typically 10-30%
Call options?	Possibly, but not for first few years after issue	Possibly, but not for first few years after issue	Possibly, but not for first few years after issue unless share price has risen to at least a test percentage of the initial conversion price	Possibly, but as for rolling-premium put convertibles	Possibly, but as for rolling-premium put convertibles
Put option(s)	No	No	Yes	Yes	Yes
Probability of eventual conversion into equity	Highest	High	Fairly high	Fairly low	Low

Put Options and the Conversion Price

The conversion price remains fixed for the life of the bond, except when the bond has a put option, giving bondholders the right to redeem their bonds above par value at any time after a specified put date.

Example
A UK company issues, at par, 5.875% convertible capital bonds on 15 June Year 1. The bonds will be due for redemption on 15 June Year 16, unless they are converted into equity. The conversion ratio is 925.93 shares per £1,000 of bonds.

The bonds have put options giving bondholders the right to redeem at 128.42 on 15 June Year 6 and 172.49 on 15 June Year 11.

Analysis
The initial conversion price is:

$$\frac{\text{Issue price}}{\text{Conversion ratio}} = \frac{£1{,}000}{925.93} = 108\text{p}$$

On the first put date on 15 June Year 6, the conversion price will increase to

$$\frac{\text{Put redemption value}}{\text{Conversion ratio}} = \frac{£1{,}284.2}{925.93} = 138.7\text{p}$$

If the bonds were not redeemed before the second put date, the conversion price would increase further on June 15 Year 11 to

$$\frac{\text{New put redemption value}}{\text{Conversion ratio}} = \frac{£1{,}724.90}{925.93} = 186.3\text{p}$$

Convertible Capital Bonds (CCBs)

Convertible capital bonds are a form of convertible bond with some distinctive features although they are similar in many respects to ordinary convertible bonds. CCBs are convertibles issued in the euromarket by a special-purpose finance subsidiary. Before they reach maturity the bonds may be exchanged for shares of the special-purpose subsidiary, and then, at the option of the bondholder, either are:

- redeemed immediately or
- exchanged for ordinary shares of the parent company.

The bonds, and interest payments on the bonds, are guaranteed by the parent company.

The parent company has the option, should it wish, of issuing convertible preferred stock in substitution for the bonds. In other words, CCBs can be structured so that they convert first into convertible preferred stock, at the option of the issuer, before they convert into equity, at the option of the investor.

Convertible Debt With Enhanced Interest

A convertible bond can be issued with an undertaking that the coupon interest rate will be increased at a date in the future if the bonds have not been converted at an earlier date.

Conversion

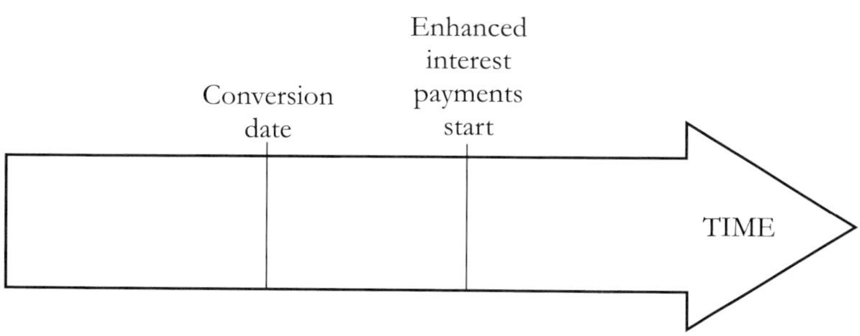

Having passed the conversion date without converting their bonds, the bondholders would start to received the higher interest. In most cases, the purpose of enhanced interest is to bring the coupon rate up to a level that the investor could have expected from investing in straight fixed-rate debt rather than the convertible bond.

Diminishing Bonds

Diminishing bonds are convertible bonds already in issue that have been steadily converted into equity by bondholders over a period, although there are some bonds outstanding that have not yet been converted or redeemed.

Exchangeable Bonds

Exchangeable bonds are very similar to convertible bonds, but with one important difference. An exchangeable bond is a bond issued by one company, giving the bondholders the right, but not the obligation, to exchange their bonds into existing shares of another company.

Exchangeable bonds might be an efficient way for the bond issuer to reduce its investment in shares of a second company without going directly to the stock market to sell the shares.

There have been a number of exchangeable bond issues involving shares in telecommunications companies. For example, Hutchison Whampoa, the Hong Kong conglomerate, issued $2.5 billion of exchangeable notes (short-term bonds) in September 2000 and a further $2.5 billion of exchangeable notes in January 2001. The notes were exchangeable into shares of the telecommunications company Vodafone. Hutchison Whampoa had acquired the Vodafone shares as payment for its stake in the German company Mannesmann that Vodafone acquired in 2000. Rather than try to sell its unwanted Vodafone shares in the stock market, and risk a heavy fall in the price of the shares, Hutchison Whampoa chose instead to issue the exchangeable bonds in the expectation that the bondholders would elect to acquire the Vodafone shares on the date for exchange.

The issue of three-year notes in September 2000 was at a coupon rate of 2.875%, each £1,000 note being exchangeable into 196.61 shares of Vodafone. The conversion price was £3.5941 and the conversion premium when the notes were issued was about 35%. In contrast, the January 2001 issue of three-year notes carried a coupon of just 2% and a conversion price of £3.10 that gave a conversion premium of about 28% at the time of the issue.

In January 2001, France Télécom issued exchangeable bonds, giving bondholders the right to exchange their bonds for shares in the telecommunications company Orange.

For an issue of exchangeable bonds to be possible, the bond issuer must hold the shares for which the bonds can be exchanged. Because there are many companies holding stakes in other companies of which they might wish to divest themselves, exchangeable bonds offer a means of disinvesting as an alternative to selling the shares on the stock market. If it were felt that a stock-market sell-off might cause a collapse in the share price, a company might prefer the option of issuing exchangeable notes or bonds.

Summary

A convertible bond is a bond that can be converted at some time into equity shares, at the choice of the bondholder. Until conversion, convertible bonds have the characteristics of straight fixed-rate bonds or liquid-yield option notes.

The right to convert the bonds into equity has a value for investors who will accept a lower rate of interest than on straight fixed-rate debt.

At the time of issuing convertible bonds, the issue price is at a premium to the current market value of the shares into which the bonds are convertible, i.e. is at a premium to parity value. This conversion premium varies in size over time, but should narrow towards zero as the conversion date approaches. This will happen only if the share price rises sufficiently between the issue date and the conversion date.

Although bonds are issued with fairly long maturities, typically 15 years in the euroconvertibles market, they are most often converted into equity or redeemed long before maturity through the exercise of a call option by the issuer or a put option by the bondholders.

Convertible bonds are issued with various specifications. Low-premium and conventional convertibles are the types of convertible most likely to be converted into equity. Convertibles with put options, including liquid-yield option notes (zero-coupon convertibles), are more likely to be redeemed early at the option of the bondholders, at a premium to par, or to the issue price in the case of liquid-yield option notes. This is because they are issued on terms that require a stronger average annual growth rate in the share price for conversion, rather than redemption, to be the preferred option for bondholders.

Convertible Bonds: Prices and Yields

Convertible bonds are fairly complex securities. There are problems measuring the yield that investors can expect to receive over time from a convertible bond. Also it can be difficult to assess the fair market value of a convertible bond.

The yield that investors in convertible bonds can expect from their investment depends on whether the bonds will be converted into shares, or if they are not converted, when they will be redeemed and at what price.

To Convert or Not to Convert?

The decision whether or not to convert bonds into equities on a conversion date will depend on:

- whether the current share price is higher than the conversion price
- whether it is the last opportunity to convert, or
- whether subsequent conversion dates will occur.

The decision faced by a convertible bondholder can be shown as a decision tree, as follows:

Decision Tree: Whether to Convert into Equity

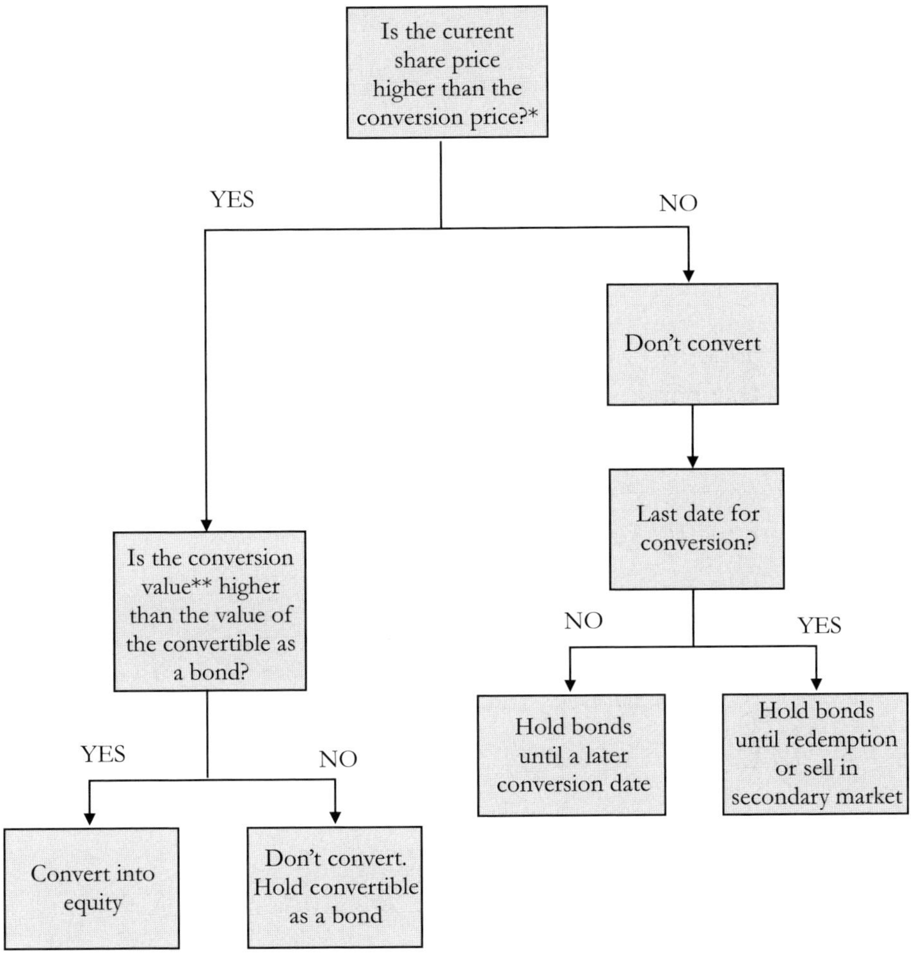

* Conversion price= redemption value of the bond divided by the number of shares into which the bond can be converted

** Conversion value = current market value of shares into which the bond can be converted, i.e. parity value

A bondholder will not convert bonds into equity shares unless the current market price of the share exceeds the conversion price. For example, if bonds can be converted into shares at a price of $5, i.e. 200

shares for every $1,000 face value of bonds, the bonds will be converted only if the market price of the share is higher than $5. If the market price is below $5, it would be cheaper to buy shares in the market.

Probability of Conversion

The probability of bondholders converting their bonds into equity depends on the terms of the issue. Low-premium and conventional convertibles have a high probability of conversion. Single-premium put convertibles and liquid-yield option notes (zero-coupon convertibles) have a much lower probability of conversion.

The probability of conversion depends on several factors:

- the conversion price
- the period of time between issue date and conversion date. The conversion date can be a long time before maturity, when the issuer has a call option on the bonds
- the expected increase in the market price of the issuer's shares
- whether the bonds are issued with a put option and, if so, the redemption price available for the put. This will affect the probability that bondholders will prefer early redemption at a premium rather than conversion into equity.

The critical factor is the anticipated and actual growth rate in the issuer's share price. In the graphs that follow, the probability that bonds will be converted is illustrated for different types of convertible bond. In each case it is assumed that the share price will grow at 5% per annum, a reasonable expectation.

Example 1
Alpha, a US company, is planning an issue of conventional convertible bonds that will be converted or redeemed in ten years. The conversion premium is 25% over the current share price of $40.

Analysis
The graph below shows:

- the conversion price
- the actual share price, assuming 5% per annum growth from the time of the bond issue to conversion date.

Probability of Conversion: Conventional Convertible Bond

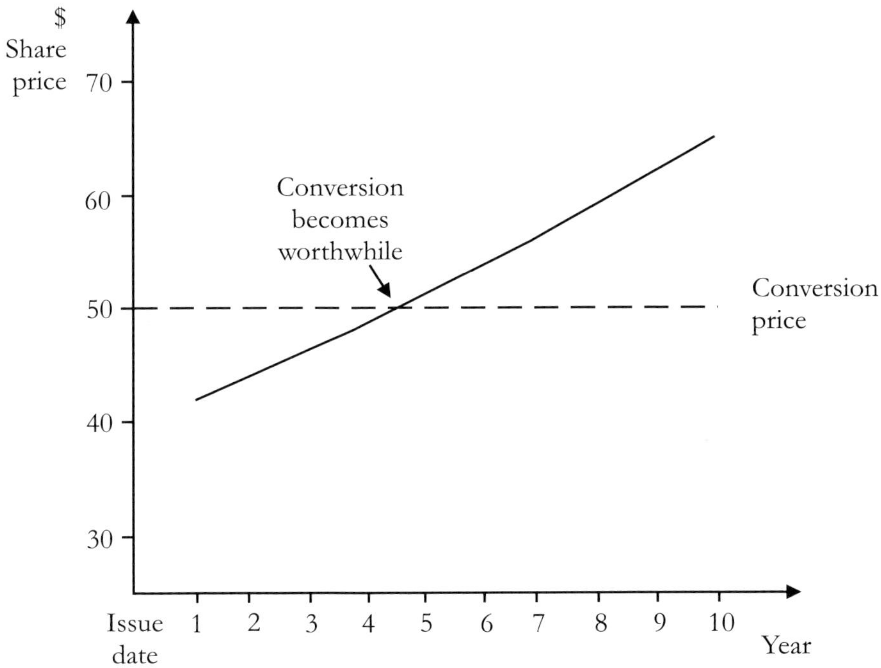

As soon as the share price rises above the conversion price, it becomes worthwhile for bondholders to convert their bonds into equity. In this example, given a share price growth of 5% per annum, conversion would become worthwhile from the fifth year onwards, and the probability of conversion at the end of ten years is high.

Example 2
Beta, a UK company, is planning the issue of premium-put convertible

bonds on the euroconvertibles market. The bonds have a 15-year maturity, but put options can be exercised after five or ten years.

The conversion price of £6 per share gives a premium on issue of 20% over the current share price of £5. The conversion ratio is 166.667 shares per £1,000 (face value) of bonds.

The put options give bondholders the right to redeem their bonds at a price that gives a yield-to-put of 8% per annum. This means that the bonds are redeemable as follows:

After 5 years	At 122.44
After 10 years	At 179.91

Analysis
The graph opposite shows:

- the conversion price
- the actual share price, assuming 5% per annum growth from the time of the bond issue to conversion date, and
- the redemption value of the bonds if the put option is exercised after five or ten years.

In this example, the share price is assumed to rise at 5% per annum. Unless the actual growth rate in the share price is higher than 5%, bondholders might decide to exercise their option to redeem after five years or after ten years. After ten years the put price of 179.91 gives the bondholders the chance to receive £1,799.10 per £1,000 face value of bonds. These bonds are convertible into 166.667 shares. This gives an equivalent share price at the put date of £10.80 (£1,799.10 ÷ 166.667). Unless the share price is higher than this, or expected to rise above £10.80, it would be more beneficial to exercise the put option than to convert the bonds into equity.

Probability of Conversion: Convertible Bond with Put Options

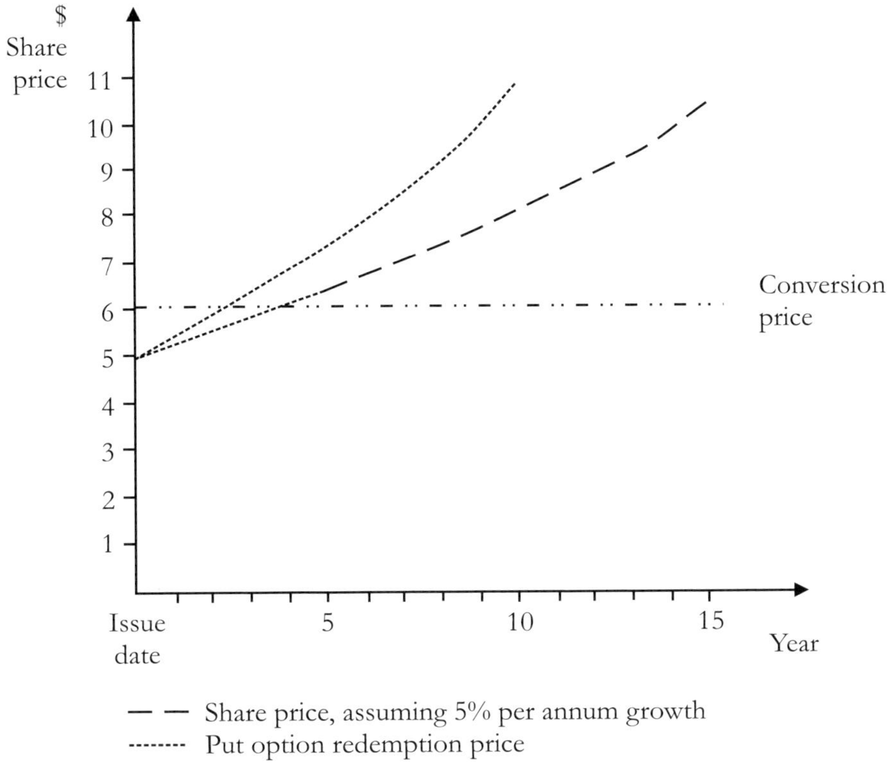

Example 3

Gamma, a US company, is planning to issue liquid-yield option notes (zero-coupon convertible bonds), redeemable at par after ten years. The issue is priced to give a 7% yield to redemption. The issue price will be \$508.35 per \$1,000 of bonds (\$1,000 ÷ $(1.07)^{10}$). There are no put or call options.

The conversion premium is 15% on issue. The share price is £6, therefore the initial conversion price is \$6.90 per share (£6 x 115%).

The conversion ratio is 73.67 shares per \$1,000 (face value) of bonds (\$508.35 ÷ \$6.90 per share). The conversion price at the redemption or conversion date has risen to \$13.57 per share (\$1,000 ÷ 73.67 shares).

Analysis
The graph below indicates:

- the conversion price at conversion date ($13.57)
- the estimated share price, assuming 5% per annum growth
- the redemption value of the bonds.

Probability of Conversion: Liquid-yield Option Note

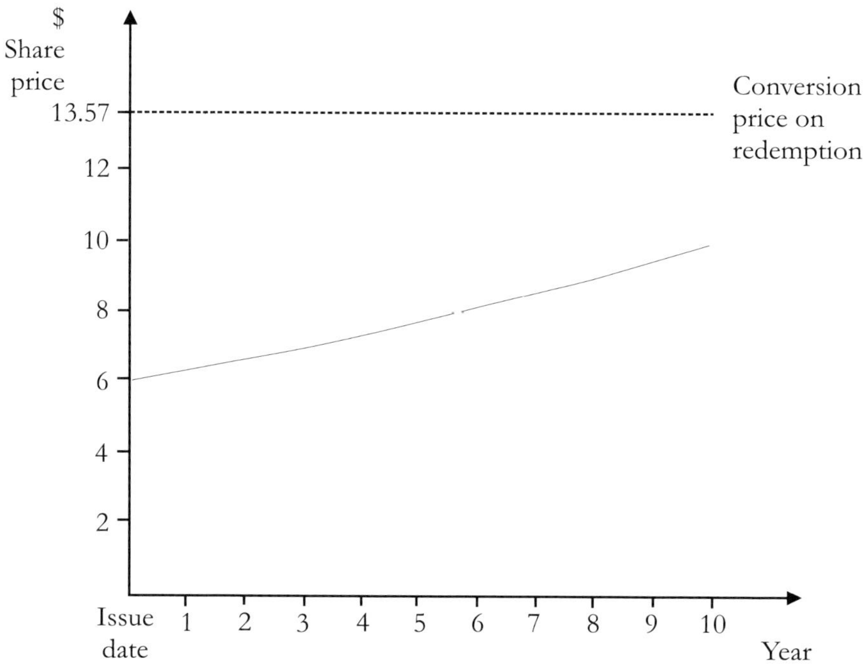

The graph shows that the bonds will be redeemed at par after ten years, and will not be converted into equity if the share price rises by only 5% per annum. This is because the redemption value of $1,000 will be higher than the market price of the shares into which they can be converted. After ten years this would be $9.77 per share, or $719.75 for 73.67 shares.

Bond Value

By the time bondholders can exercise their right to convert their bonds into equity, they will do so only if the value of the shares into which the bonds can be converted exceeds the value of the convertibles as straight bonds.

Suppose for example that bondholders have the right to convert every $100 of their convertible bonds into 40 shares; otherwise the bonds would be redeemed immediately at par.

- If the current price of the shares is more than $2.50, more than $100 in total per $100 of bonds, the bondholders will convert the bonds into equity.
- If the shares are worth less than $2.50 each, less than $100 in total per $100 of bonds, the bondholders would redeem their bonds. If they want to buy shares in the company, it would be cheaper to do so in the market at a price below $2.50.

Example
A company issued 5% convertible bonds ten years ago, giving bondholders the right to convert into equity at the ratio of 30 shares for each $100 of bonds.

A conversion date has been reached and bondholders can now exercise their right to convert. The share price is $4.

It has been estimated that if bondholders held on to their 5% bonds until maturity, the value of the bonds as straight debt would be $97 per cent.

Analysis
The market price of the convertibles would have risen as the company's share price went up. The convertibles are worth only $97 per cent as straight debt, but they are worth $120 per cent (30 shares x $4 per share) on conversion into equity. In this example, the current market price of the convertibles should be at least 120. It should be even higher if the right to convert can be made at a later date because the share price could rise above $4 before then.

Measuring Bond Value

The bond value of a convertible is the estimated market value it would have as a straight fixed-rate bond. Straight bond values are calculated by discounting the future interest and principal payments on the bond, either:

- to maturity, or
- up to a date when the bond would be called by the issuer.

The interest rate used for discounting should be the yield the company would expect to pay on straight debt with the same coupon and same maturity.

Example

Alpha plc, a UK company, has issued 4% convertible bonds. These are convertible into equity shares of Alpha at a conversion price of 360p. If they are not converted, the bonds will be redeemed at par after five years. Interest is paid annually.

Investors in straight fixed-rate bonds would expect a yield of 5.5% per annum on bonds with a five-year maturity.

Analysis

The bond value of the convertibles can be calculated by discounting to a present value the future interest payments and the repayment of debt principal at maturity. The discount rate to apply to the interest payments and repayment of principal is $1/(1 + r)^n$ where:

- r is the annual yield that investors wish to receive, as a proportion, on straight bonds with the same maturity as the convertible, and
- n is the number of time periods after which the income will be received.

Because interest payments are annual rather than semi-annual, r, the annual yield on straight five-year bonds, is 0.055 (= 5.5%) and n represents the number of years before each item of income will be received.

Bond Value of 4% Convertible Bond (per £100 face value)

	n	Item	Amount	Discount factor	Present value
			£		£
After 1 year	1	Interest	4	$1/(1.055)^1$	3.79
After 2 years	2	Interest	4	$1/(1.055)^2$	3.59
After 3 years	3	Interest	4	$1/(1.055)^3$	3.41
After 4 years	4	Interest	4	$1/(1.055)^4$	3.23
After 5 years	5	Interest	4	$1/(1.055)^5$	3.06
After 5 years	5	Capital payment	100	$1/(1.055)^5$	76.51
				Bond value	93.59

The bond value of the convertible is 93.59. In other words, if the convertible were a straight bond, without the rights of conversion into equity, the value of the bond would be 93.59.

The bond value of a convertible is not fixed, but can fluctuate:

- with changes in market rates of interest, i.e. bond yields, and
- as the bond approaches maturity and redemption.

When market interest rates (bond yields) fall, bond values will rise. When bond yields rise, the market price of bonds will fall. As a bond approaches its redemption date, its value becomes less susceptible to interest-rate changes. Its market value moves towards the amount of the redemption payment. If a bond is redeemable at par, for example, its market value will move towards par as the redemption date approaches and will be at par on redemption.

Bond Premium

The bond value of a convertible is the minimum price it will have at any time. However, a convertible's current market value can exceed its bond value, and there can be a bond premium. The bond premium is simply the difference between the market value of the convertible and its bond value, i.e. its value as straight debt, and it represents the extra amount that bondholders are willing to pay above a straight bond price for the conversion rights.

The bond premium can be expressed as an option cost per share or a rights premium per share, as follows:

$$\text{Rights premium per share} = \frac{\text{Bond premium}}{\text{Conversion ratio}}$$

Example
A convertible bond has a current market price of 112. Its bond value as straight fixed-rate debt would be 97. The conversion ratio is 45 shares per $100 of convertible bonds.

Analysis
The bond premium per $100 of bonds is $15 (112-97). The rights premium per share, the extra that bondholders are willing to pay for their right to convert into equity at a future date, is $0.33 per share ($15 ÷ 45 shares).

Minimum Price

The minimum price of a convertible bond always should be the lower amount of:

- its current value as a straight bond earning a fixed rate of interest to maturity, and
- the current market value of the shares into which it can be converted.

The diagram opposite shows the minimum price of a convertible over time, on the assumption that the market price of the share rises at a steady rate between the issue of the bond and its conversion date.

Minimum Price of a Convertible

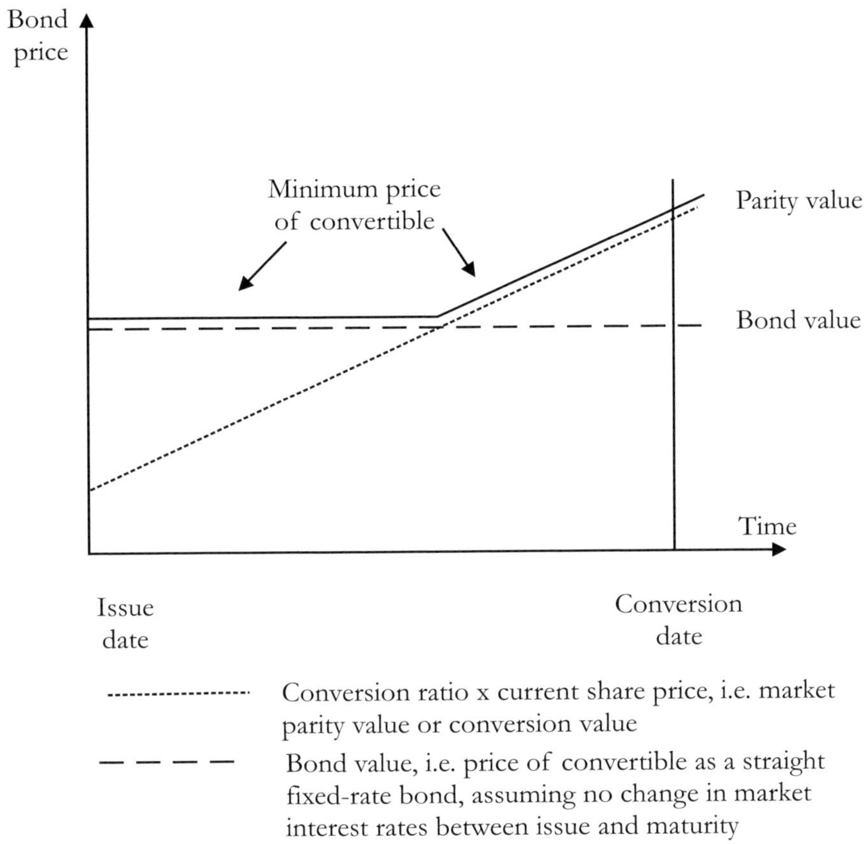

As the share price rises, the minimum conversion premium narrows to a point where the convertible's price is determined by equity share prices rather than the convertible's value as a straight bond.

Share Price Falls

Convertibles will attract investors only if there is an expectation that share prices will rise between issue date and conversion date.

Whenever share prices fall, convertibles will cease to be attractive.

- The price of existing convertibles will fall towards their bond value, i.e. their value as straight fixed-rate debt.
- If convertibles have put options, these will be exercised by bondholders who will redeem the bonds and switch into higher-yielding investments.
- It may be difficult for companies to make new convertibles issues unless the prospects for share prices improve, and there are expectations or a likelihood of a share price recovery.

When share prices fall, conversion premiums will rise to very high levels, because of the fall in the parity value of the shares.

Example
Delta issued $100 million of convertible bonds at par. The conversion price was $7.45, so that the conversion ratio was 134.23 shares per $1,000 of bonds (1,000 ÷ 7.45). At the time of the issue, the share price was $6.

Four years later, the share price had fallen to $4.50 following trading difficulties. The market price of the convertible had fallen to 98.0.

Analysis
The conversion premium on issue was 24.1%, as follows:

	$
Issue price	1,000.00
Parity value (134.23 shares x $6)	805.38
Premium	194.62

Conversion premium = 24.1% (194.62 ÷ 805.38 x 100%).

However, four years later, because of the fall in the share price and despite a small fall in the price of the convertible, the conversion premium is much higher.

	$
Market price per $1,000 of bonds	980.00
Parity value (134.23 shares x $4.50)	604.04
Premium	375.96

Conversion premium = 62.2% (375.96 ÷ 604.04 x 100%).

Unless there is a substantial increase in the share price before the conversion date for the bonds, the bonds will not be converted into equity.

Exercise

To check that you understand the decision whether or not to convert, attempt your own solution to this problem.

Gamma has issued convertible bonds with a single-premium put option. The conversion price is 480¢. At the put option's exercise date the share price is 510¢. The put option gives bondholders the right to redeem their bonds at 120. If the put option is not exercised, the bond will be callable at any time by Gamma at par.

What should the bondholders do at the put option exercise date?

Solution

The conversion price is 480¢, therefore the conversion ratio is 208.333 shares per $1,000 nominal value of bonds $1,000 ÷ 480¢ per share. The conversion value of these shares at the put option exercise date is $1,062.50 (208.333 x 510¢).

In effect, this is the last date for conversion because if bondholders do no convert, and do not exercise their put option, Gamma will exercise its call option and redeem the bonds at par.

The decision tree can be shown as follows:

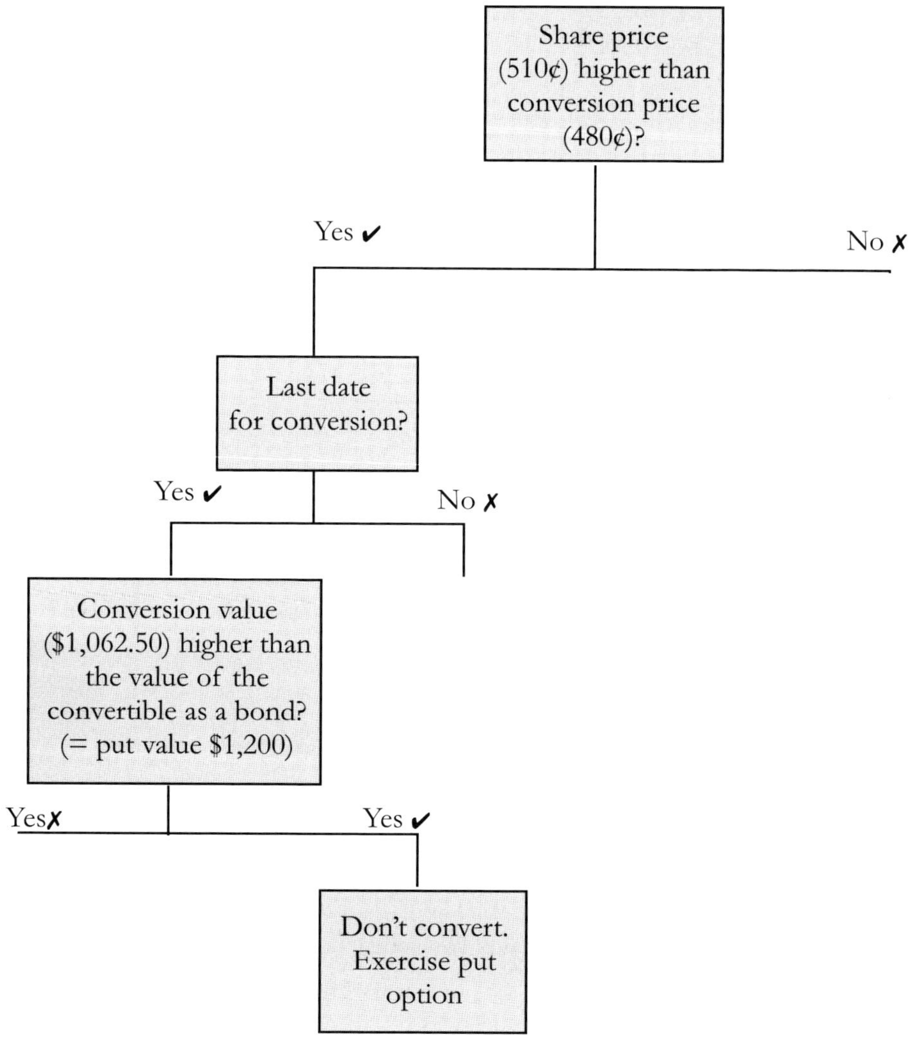

Yield

The yield on an investment is the annual rate of return to the investor, measured as a percentage of the investment's market value. In the case of bonds, the return to investors comes from the annual interest payments and the redemption of the debt principal at maturity. In the case of equity shares, return can be measured as the annual dividend plus any increase in the share price, or minus any fall in the price, during the investment period.

Measuring the return on a convertible bond is more complicated. The complications arise for two main reasons.

- *The hybrid nature of a convertible.* In the short term, return consists of interest, but in the longer term the return will depend on whether the bond is converted into equity or redeemed. If eventually the bond is converted, equity yields – dividends and share price growth – are relevant to the measurement of return.
- *Uncertainty about the redemption date.* If the bond has a call option or put option, there will be some uncertainty, if the bond is redeemed, about *when* it will be redeemed and at what price.

The yield on convertible bonds can be reported in any of the following ways:

- as a yield to redemption
- as a yield to put
- by providing information about the investment performance of the company's equity shares.

Yield to Redemption

The minimum yield from a convertible is the yield that the bondholder will obtain if the bonds are not converted but are redeemed at maturity. This is the redemption yield on the bond.

The yield to redemption is the average annual return from a bond, as a percentage of its current market value, that an investor will receive if the bond is held until maturity, and then redeemed.

Example

A convertible bond has a current market price of 102. If the bonds are not converted, they will be redeemed at par in five years. The coupon rate is 8%, with interest payable every six months.

Analysis

The yield on the bond could be measured as a current yield or a redemption yield.

The current yield is the annual interest receivable each year, as a percentage of the current market price. In this example, the current yield is 7.84% (8/102 x 100%).

The redemption yield, or maturity yield, is an average annual rate of return on the current market cost of the investment. The redemption yield takes into consideration both the interest yield and the capital gain or loss on redemption.

In this example, the redemption yield on the convertible is about 7.5% per annum (workings not shown). It is slightly below the current yield because there is a capital loss of 2 (102-100) on redemption because the bonds would be redeemed at par. The capital loss represents a negative yield.

Yield to Put

When a convertible bond has a put option, there is a distinct possibility that it will be redeemed at the next put date (put option exercise date). The yield to put is the yield that bondholders will receive measured against the current market value of the convertible, if they redeem their bonds at the next put date. The yield consists of both interest receivable to the put date and the redemption value of the bond at that date.

Example

Beta, a UK company, has issued sterling convertible bonds on the euroconvertibles market. The coupon rate of interest is 5%, payable annually. The bonds are convertible into equity shares of Beta at a conversion price of 440p, but there is also a put option. Bondholders can redeem their bonds in two years at a price of 122.5. The current market price of the convertible is 111.90.

Analysis

The yield to put is the average annual rate of return that the bondholder will receive on an investment of £111.90, from annual interest payments of £5 each year for two years and a payment on redemption after two years at £122.50.

This yield is the discount rate at which the interest and debt principal payments have a present value equal to the market price of the convertible. In this example, it is 9% per annum, as shown in the table below. The yield to put is 9%, making the discount factor $1/(1.09)^n$.

	n	Item	Amount	Discount factor $1/(1 + r)^n$	Present value
			£		£
After 1 year	1	Interest	6	$1/(1.09)^1$	4.59
After 2 years	2	Interest	6	$1/(1.09)^2$	4.21
After 2 years	5	Payment on redemption	122.5	$1/(1.09)^2$	103.10
		Market value of convertible			111.90

Equity Yields

The yield for investors in a convertible bond will change from bond yields – current and redemption yields – to equity yields if eventually the bonds are converted.

- There will be an increase in the capital value of the investment as the share price rises.
- After conversion, the annual yield on the equity shares will consist of a dividend plus the yield from any continuing increase in the market price of the shares, i.e. dividends plus capital gain.

Prior to the conversion date, bondholders should monitor historical yields on equity as a means of predicting future performance.

Market Prices

A convertible bond's market value is the price at which the bond can be issued in the primary market or resold to a willing buyer in the secondary market. Prices are quoted in the same way as for bonds, in relation to a par value of 100.

The minimum price of a convertible should be its bond value, but a convertible bond's market price might be at or close to its bond value if it is unlikely that the bond will ever be converted into equity. If there were a possibility that the bonds could be converted into equity, their market value should reflect what investors think will happen to the share price.

Example
A company has issued convertible bonds. The coupon rate is 4.5%, and the bonds are either redeemable at par in two years' time or convertible into equity at a conversion ratio of 20 shares per $1,000 of bonds. The current share price is $48.

Analysis
At the current share price, holders of the convertible bonds would not convert them into equity because the parity value of the shares per $1,000 of bonds is just $960 (20 x $48).

The market price of the bond should be not less than its value as a fixed-rate bond with a 4.5% coupon and two years to maturity. Investors might believe, however, that the share price will rise during the next two years, and that the bond probably will be converted into equity. The market price of the convertible bond should be higher than its bond value; just how much higher will depend on what investors think will happen to the share price, i.e. how high will the price rise before conversion date, and how confident are investors about this prediction?

This example helps to illustrate the uncertainty about what the price of a convertible bond should be. The same uncertainty applies to market valuations of equity prices.

A theoretical price can be established for a convertible, just as a theoretical price can be established for equity shares.

- Investors can compare their estimate of a theoretical price with the current market price, and buy or sell convertible bonds according to whether they believe the market price to be low or high.
- An issuer of convertible bonds and its advisers, can use a model for calculating a theoretical price to help when making a decision about what the issue price should be.

A Pricing Model

The price of a convertible bond should be either its value as a straight bond, or its value as equity, whichever is the higher.

However, its value as a bond should include a premium over the bond value and its value as equity should include a premium over the conversion value.

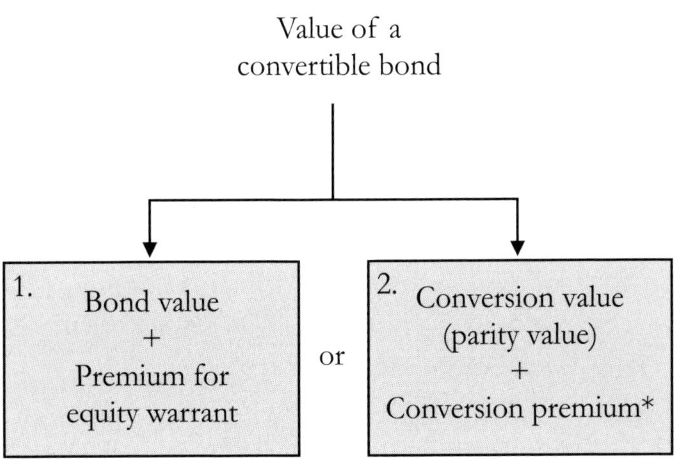

A convertible's value should be whichever is the higher of 1. or 2.

** A conversion premium arises because bondholders receive a current yield in the form of annual interest that is higher than the dividend yield they would receive if they held equity shares. (Current yields on bonds normally are higher than dividend yields.)*

Value as a Bond

The market value of a convertible bond as a straight bond should be:

- its bond value, plus
- a premium for the benefit of the option to convert into equities.

A market value can be estimated for the premium for the option to convert using a mathematical pricing model. The approach to valuation is broadly similar to pricing a share warrant. (A share warrant is a right to subscribe for equity shares in a company at a future date and at a fixed price. Warrants, and their valuation, are described in Chapter 7.)

Value as Equity

The value of a convertible bond as equity should be:

- its parity value or conversion value, i.e. the current market value of the shares into which the bond can be converted, plus
- a premium for the value to bondholders of the downside income protection provided by the fixed-rate interest income and the ability to redeem the bonds, if required, at a fixed price. This is the conversion premium.

Estimating a value for the conversion premium could be based on measurements of current conversion premiums on convertibles in the secondary market. There are different estimating techniques, the simplest being the concept of breakeven or payback.

Breakeven or Payback

The interest yield or current yield, on a bond normally is higher than dividend yields on equity shares. This is because not all profits are paid to shareholders as dividends and dividends can be low in spite of the company being profitable. Some profits are retained for reinvestment and should help the company to achieve profits growth in future.

Profit growth should result in higher dividends and higher share prices. Dividend yields will remain low, even when dividends are increasing.

This is because the share price also is rising and the dividend yield is the annual dividend as a percentage of the share price. In comparing bond yields and equity dividend yields, it should be expected that bond yields will be higher.

Breakeven for a convertible bond, also known as payback, is the number of years it would take the bondholder to recover the cost of the conversion premium out of the higher-interest yield on the bond compared with the current dividend yield from equity shares.

Example
A $100 bond is convertible into 20 shares. The current market price of the bond is 105 and the share price is $4.50. The current yield on the bond is 7.5% per annum and the current dividend yield is 5% per annum.

Analysis
Convertible bondholders are willing to pay a conversion premium for the bonds rather than buy equity shares. The conversion premium is:

	$
Market price of convertible	105
Parity value of shares (20 x $4.50)	90
Premium	15
Premium as a percentage (15 ÷ 90 x 100%)	16.7%

The bondholders receive the advantage of a higher income from the bonds (7.5%) compared with the dividend yield from investing in equity (5%). This income advantage of 2.5% per annum can be compared with the conversion premium of 16.7%.

Formula for Simple Breakeven
The formula for payback or simple breakeven is:

$$\frac{\text{Conversion premium}}{(\text{Current yield on bond} - \text{Dividend yield on shares})}$$

In the example above, payback is

$$\frac{16.7\%}{(7.5\% - 5\%)} = \frac{16.7}{2.5} = 6.7 \text{ years}$$

This formula is simple and crude. It takes no account of the difference between the market price of the convertible on which the current yield is being earned, and the parity value of the shares to which the dividend yield should apply. Nevertheless, the concept of simple breakeven can be used:

- by investors to assess the value of a convertible, and
- by issuers to assist with deciding the terms of a new convertible bond issue.

Typically, investors in convertible bonds might look for a fairly quick breakeven, perhaps of no more than three years, although a longer breakeven would be acceptable for convertibles with a high bond value, and breakeven periods also will vary with current conditions in the market for convertible bonds..

Example

Delta, a US company, is planning the issue of 5.5% convertible bonds. The current market price of Delta's shares is $50 and the current dividend yield is 2.5%. The bond issue will be at par. Delta's management and advisers believe the payback on issue should not be higher than four years.

Analysis

The bond will have a coupon yield of 5.5%. This also will be the current yield if the bond is issued at par. The maximum premium on issue can be established from the maximum payback.

$$\frac{\text{Conversion Premium}}{\text{Current yield - Dividend yield}} = \text{Payback}$$

$$\frac{\text{Conversion Premium}}{(5.5\% - 2.5\%)} = 4 \text{ years (max.)}$$

Conversion Premium = 4 x 3.0% max

= 12.0% max

If the conversion premium should not exceed 12%, the parity value of the shares on issue, per $1,000 of bonds, should be not less than

$1,000 x 100/112 = $892.56

The current share price is $50 and the conversion ratio should be not less than:

$$\frac{\text{Parity value}}{\text{Current share price}} = \frac{\$892.56}{\$50} = 17.8512 \text{ shares per } \$1{,}000 \text{ bonds}$$

This suggests a maximum conversion price of $56.02 ($1,000 ÷ 17.8512).

The company can decide to offer the bonds with a conversion price of $56, giving a conversion premium of 12% over the current share price of $50. Payback would be 4.0 years (12% ÷ 3.0%).

Derivatives and Convertible Bonds

As explained earlier, the value of a convertible can be analyzed as its value as a straight bond and the value of the equity conversion rights. There has been a growing use of *derivative instruments* to strip out the equity option from the straight bond and to sell it separately. Investors can choose to invest in the conversion rights only, or to invest in the bond rights only.

Summary

There is a direct relationship for any security between yield and price. Yields on investments vary over time with changes in market conditions, for example, as a result of government economic policy or in response to changes in the rate of inflation.

When the required yield from a security goes up, the price at which it is traded in the market will fall. When required yields fall, the price at which a security is traded will rise.

Changes in yields have several consequences:

- Existing holders of securities will benefit from a rise or suffer a fall in the market value of their investment.
- Companies wishing to issue new securities will have to offer a higher or lower price on issue, or a higher or lower coupon yield.
- Investors in a new issue of securities will expect to receive yield that reflects the new market rate.

There are some difficulties in measuring yields on convertible bonds, however:

- Yields can be measured in different ways, depending on the probability of eventual conversion into equity and on the expected date of redemption, and the redemption value.
- Market prices often include a premium over the value of the convertibles as straight debt and over their current conversion value into equity shares. A suitable market price can be estimated either by adding a premium valuation to bond value or by using a breakeven pricing model to calculate a premium over conversion value.

Why Use Convertibles?

Convertibles are not used as widely as equity or straight-debt securities for raising capital, but in some situations they can meet the differing requirements of a company wishing to raise capital and of investors wishing to add to their investment portfolio.

Reasons for Issuing Convertibles

A company's reasons for issuing convertible bonds depend to a large extent on whether it expects the bonds to be converted into equity.

If the company thinks it is probable that the bondholders will convert their bonds into equity, the convertibles could be regarded as *delayed equity*, in which case the reasons for issuing the convertibles might be:

- to raise the equity capital early at a premium to its current price, or
- to raise capital as convertibles rather than equity because the current share price is considered too low.

If a company raised capital by issuing new equity shares, the issue price would have to be near the market price for existing shares, or, in the case of a rights issue to existing shareholders, at a discount of 15-20% to the current market price. Convertible bonds, in contrast, would be issued at a conversion premium over the current share market price. As a consequence, the company would be raising capital in a way that limits the number of new shares that might be created on conversion, and thereby restricts the possible dilution of equity.

Example

Alpha's current share price is 400¢. It wishes to raise $120 million, either through a rights issue of shares or by issuing convertible bonds. The bonds would be issued at a price that gives a conversion premium of 20% on issue. A rights issue price would be at a 10% discount to the current market price.

Analysis

To make a rights issue at a price of 360¢ per share (400¢ less 10%) the company would have to issue 33.33 million shares ($120 million ÷ $3.60) to raise $120 million. These shares would entitle their owners to dividend payments from the time of issue.

If the company opted to issue convertible bonds at par, the conversion price would be 480¢ per share, giving a premium of 20% over the current market price. The terms of the bond issue would be to offer 208.3333 shares on conversion for every $1,000 of bonds, as follows:

Conversion price (120% of 400¢)	=	$4.80 per share
Number of shares issuable at this price ($120m ÷ $4.80)	=	25 million
Conversion ratio (25 million shares ÷ $120m)	=	208.3333 shares per $1,000 bonds

After conversion, assuming that all the bonds eventually are converted into equity, there would be fewer extra shares in issue than if the capital had been raised by means of a rights issue. The company would be obliged to pay fixed-rate interest on the convertibles until conversion takes place.

If the company thought it unlikely that an issue of convertibles would be converted into equity, its reason for making the issue would be to raise low-cost debt finance. The coupon on convertibles is lower than for straight fixed-rate debt with the same maturity.

Advantages of convertible bonds for the issuer can be:

- a means of issuing an unsecured bond when it has insufficient assets for a secured bond

- the low after-tax cost of borrowing in the years up to redemption or conversion.

Convertible bonds have a lower after-tax cost than equity. Interest payments are an allowable expense for the purpose of calculating taxable profits, whereas share dividends are not allowable. Convertible bonds also have a lower interest cost than straight fixed-rate bonds because they can be issued at a lower coupon.

The Risk of Refinancing at Redemption

Companies that issue convertible bonds could expect that the bonds eventually will be converted into equity, and so will never have to be redeemed. If the share price does not rise sufficiently before conversion date the bondholders will not convert into equity and will expect the bonds to be redeemed.

A potential risk for the bond issuer is that to redeem the convertibles, it could be forced to raise new debt capital, possibly at a higher cost than it has been paying on the convertibles.

The Japanese bond markets in the late 1980s and early 1990s provide an interesting example of this risk for convertible bond issuers. A number of Japanese companies issued convertibles before the collapse in share prices on the Tokyo Stock Exchange in 1989. As a consequence of the slump in share prices, holders of the convertible bonds chose to redeem the bonds rather than convert them into equity. This created problems for the issuers who had to find ways of raising new capital to pay for the redemption of the bonds.

A number of Japanese banks experienced the same problem, but with the extra problem of currency risk. Some banks issued Swiss-franc-denominated convertibles with put options in the late 1980s, to mature around 1992-1994. The collapse in Japanese share prices in 1989 made the terms of conversion unattractive to bondholders who elected to exercise their put option, typically at a 5% to 10% premium to par value to compound the problem, the yen weakened in value against the Swiss franc over the period of the issue. This added to the overall cost in yen of the bonds, the banks having to pay more in yen, first to pay interest on the bonds, and finally to redeem their Swiss-franc bonds.

Reasons for Investing in Convertibles

For investors, convertible bonds can combine the attractive features of bonds and equities.

They offer the low-risk features of bonds.

- The market value of a convertible should not fall below the market value of a straight fixed-rate bond with the same coupon and maturity date, although this market price could rise or fall in response to changes in market rates of interest.
- The market value of a convertible with a put option could be enhanced by the redemption value for the put.
- With the exception of zero-coupon bonds, convertible bonds pay an annual income to the investor in the form of interest.
- There are some risks when investing in convertibles and in bonds generally, but bond investments usually represent a lower risk than equity investments. Risks are explained below.

The coupon rate for convertibles will be lower than for fixed-rate bonds issued at the same time and for the same maturity. Convertibles, however, offer a higher potential return in the long term than straight bonds because of the equity conversion rights they give to the bondholder. Convertible bondholders enjoy some of the upside potential of investing in equities because they have the opportunity to benefit from the company's success and any large increase in its share price.

At worst, convertibles are a low-coupon bond. At best, they are a long-term growth stock, for which investors pay a premium, in the form of a conversion premium, to acquire the equity.

Convertibles also may be an attractive investment when equity prices are uncertain. For example, after a fall in share prices in most of the world's stock markets during 2000, there was strong renewed interest in convertibles. Investing in convertibles gives the investor the opportunity to benefit from a share price recovery while still enjoying some interest income. In contrast, investing directly in shares puts the investor at risk of further share price falls and a low or negative investment return.

Financial Risks from Investing in Convertibles

The risks attached to investing in convertibles are similar to those facing investors in bonds or equities. The main risks are:

- credit risk
- event risk
- changes in market interest rates
- liquidity in the secondary market
- saturation of the convertibles market
- a downturn in the company's profits and share price.

Credit risk refers to the possibility that the issuer of the bonds will fail to make interest payments on schedule, or will be unable to redeem the bonds if asked to do so by the bondholders, either at maturity or at a put option exercise date. The scale of the credit risk will be reflected in the credit rating for the bonds. Investors can minimize their credit risk by investing in investment-grade bonds rather than in high-yield junk bonds.

Event risk refers to the possibility of events occurring that will affect the company's financial position and its ability to honor its obligations. These may be referred to as restructuring events and may include a takeover of the company or a disposal of a major part of the company's business. Convertibles should be issued with a provision giving bondholders either the right to demand immediate redemption of their bonds, should such an event occur, or the right to a lower conversion price for the shares, i.e. a higher conversion ratio, the bonds being made convertible into a larger number of shares.

Investors in convertible bonds and any other bonds, are exposed to some *price risk*. This is the risk of a fall in the market price of their bond.

The market price of convertible bonds, like the price of straight bonds, responds to changes in market interest rates. When market interest rates go up, bond prices fall, and equity prices usually fall too.

Investors often are reluctant to purchase securities if there is an *illiquid secondary market.* In a liquid market they would be able to sell their securities at any time easily and at a fair price. In an illiquid market, it is difficult to find a willing buyer, and bondholders could be forced to hold onto their bonds or to sell at a low price. Unless an investor in convertibles knows that he/she will hold them until conversion or redemption, he/she faces the risk of a loss on reselling the investment in an illiquid market.

There is a risk that when there is an abnormally large volume of new-issue activity, the market will become *saturated,* with too many issuers chasing too few investors. In a saturated market, bond yields will fall, and conversion premiums also will be made lower to attract investors.

A downturn in the profits of an issuer of convertible bonds probably will result in a fall in the issuer's share price. The probability of investors converting their bonds into shares may fall as a result, and the price of the convertible also would fall, increasing the conversion premium.

Convertibles and Takeovers

Convertible bonds or preference shares can provide a suitable method of financing the acquisition of another company in cases where the acquired company is:

- quite large relative to the size of the buying company, and
- owned mainly by a single individual or group of closely related individuals.

If the buying company cannot pay in cash, it might have to finance the acquisition by paying the shareholders of the acquired company in newly issued shares or bonds. If it paid for the subsidiary with equity shares, it might pass control or influence over its affairs to the sellers who immediately would become a major shareholder.

Negotiated terms for the takeover might involve the selling shareholders agreeing to take some or all of the payment in convertible bonds from the buyer. Payment in convertible bonds or convertible preference shares would give the seller some security of a fixed income, and the opportunity to join in the long-term growth of the company by converting the bonds or shares into equity at a future date.

Example

Sierra, an organization with 10 million shares in issue, wishes to buy Tango, a company with six million shares. The market price of Sierra's shares is $3 and the agreed price for the takeover is $2 for each of Tango's shares. Tango is almost entirely owned by a single person.

Sierra is short of cash, and wishes to pay for the takeover by issuing shares or bonds.

Analysis

The market value of Sierra is $30 million. The agreed value of Tango is $12 million. To buy Tango with equity shares, Sierra would have to issue four million shares ($12 million ÷ $3 per share) and almost all would be owned by a single person who would own over 28% (4 million ÷ 14 million x 100%) of Sierra.

This is likely be unacceptable to Sierra's board of directors and its shareholders.

An alternative offer could be to pay for Tango with 6% convertible bonds with a conversion price of $3.50. The payment could be as follows:

	Value $ million
1 million ordinary shares in Sierra	3.0
$9 million of 6% convertible bonds	9.0
	12.0

By the time the conversion date is reached, Sierra could have become larger and could have issued more shares, so reducing the size of the single owner's stake in the organization.

A convertible bond also might be used to pay for the acquisition of a company with low earnings, in order to avoid a dilution in the earnings per share of the buying company.

Example
One company, Echo, wishes to acquire another company, Foxtrot, for $100 million. Foxtrot is a young company, and its pre-tax profits are still quite small at $4 million. Profits are expected to rise in the future, and Foxtrot's shareholders want to participate in the growth of the business by holding some equity in Echo. Echo has annual earnings of $200 million, and its directors are concerned that if it purchased Foxtrot by issuing new shares, there would be an unacceptable dilution for a year or so in the earnings per share of Echo.

A solution to the problem might be to pay the Foxtrot shareholders in convertible notes or bonds. Provided the interest cost on the bonds does not exceed the profits generated by Foxtrot's business ($4 million per annum, or 4%), there would be no reduction in the earnings of Echo after the takeover, and no dilution in earnings per share.

Before conversion of the bonds into equity takes place, there should be time for the enlarged group to build up profitability.

5

The Convertible Bond Markets

Convertible bonds can be issued and traded in any domestic stock market. There is also an international market, the euroconvertibles market. Euroconvertibles include convertible preferred stock as well as convertible bonds. The main domestic markets for convertibles are the US, Switzerland and Japan.

Euroconvertibles Market

The euromarket for convertible bonds operates in a similar way to the eurobond and euroequities markets. The bonds are issued in several international centers at the same time, and distributed internationally by a syndicate of securities houses and investment banks.

For each issue, the company appoints a lead manager. This is a securities house or investment bank that:

- advises on the issue
- assembles an international syndicate to underwrite and sell the issue
- appoints a paying agent in each of two or three countries that is responsible for paying interest to bondholders
- makes a secondary market in the bonds after issue. Dealers in other international centers also could act as dealers in a secondary market.

The main financial centers for issuing and trading euroconvertibles are London and Switzerland.

The most common types of euroconvertible issue are conventional convertibles and convertibles with put options. Most issues of both types have call options. Issuers are large multinational companies. The main buyers are institutional investors, including both equity funds and fixed-income funds. Interest on euroconvertibles is paid gross, without deduction of any withholding tax at source by the bond issuer.

Foreign Currency Issues

A company can issue euroconvertibles in any freely traded currency. When the currency of the bonds is different from the currency of the shares into which the bonds may be converted, the conversion price is fixed in both the currency of issue and the currency in which the shares are traded. The terms of the issue must specify a fixed rate of exchange between the currencies for the purpose of conversion.

Example

A UK-based multinational issues 5.5% convertible capital bonds in dollars. The conversion price on issue is $3.45 with a fixed rate of £1 = $1. 50.

The bonds are convertible into equity shares of the company at a conversion ratio of 289.855 shares for each $1,000 of bonds ($1,000 ÷ $3.45 per share). The conversion price in sterling is £2.30 ($3.45 ÷ $1.50 to £1).

Maturity

Most euroconvertible issues to date have had a final maturity of 15 years. However, many issues have put options, so the effective maturity is often as short as the first put option exercise date, typically five years after issue.

Coupon

The coupon rate payable on euroconvertibles varies according to the currency. Most often coupons are fixed at an amount somewhere between the coupon that would be paid on straight fixed-rate debt with the same maturity in the same currency, and the current dividend yield on the issuer's shares.

Call Options

Many euroconvertible issues have a provisional call option that allows the issuer to redeem the bonds, unless they are converted immediately, but only if the share price has risen to a certain amount. The share price that triggers the issuer's right to call the bond typically is set at about 130% to 150% of the initial conversion price.

Generally euroconvertible issues also give the issuer an absolute call option after several years from the issue date.

US Domestic Market

The US domestic market for convertible bonds largely is confined to US issuers. However, the adoption of Rule 144A by the Securities and Exchange Commission (SEC) in 1990 opened up the US market to foreign issuers.

Rule 144A of the Securities Act relaxed the restrictions on the issue and resale of unregistered securities, i.e. securities that are not registered with the SEC before issue. The requirement to register issues with the SEC had been a major restraint on foreign companies accessing the US market. The market in unregistered securities, known as the private placement market, is now open to US and foreign issuers of bonds, notes, equities or convertibles. Issues of convertibles, like issues of bonds, notes or commercial paper in the US, should have a credit rating.

A problem for foreign issuers of convertibles in the US markets is the liquidity of the market for their equity shares. For example, if a UK-listed company wished to raise capital from an issue of convertibles, the private placement market (the 144A market) would not be a serious option unless its equity shares are traded on the market or on a stock exchange such as New York in the US. American investors generally will be reluctant to buy convertibles of a foreign issuer if the only market for the shares is in Europe or Japan, for example.

The maturity to redemption of US convertible issues typically is 20 to 25 years. Convertibles issued in the US usually have call options. Put options, however, have been fairly unusual.

Sinking Funds

Most issues of conventional convertibles in the US provide for a sinking fund. The issuer makes an annual payment into the fund, and the money in the fund is invested until used to buy back the convertible bonds in the market. After repurchase, the bonds are retired, or canceled. Payments into a sinking funds are set at an amount sufficient to retire about 70 to 80% of convertibles before maturity or conversion.

Euroconvertible Market Regulations and Procedures

Like the eurobond market, the euroconvertibles market is self-regulated, and has two regulatory bodies, the International Securities Market Association (ISMA) and the International Primary Markets Association (IPMA).

ISMA is based in Zurich, its members deal in the international capital markets. It provides a regulatory framework for the secondary international markets, and has established uniform practises that govern secondary-market transactions in international securities such as eurobonds. It also was responsible for introducing a computerized trading system for eurobonds (TRAX).

IPMA is a trade association of the leading underwriters in the *primary* international capital markets. Like ISMA, it is a self-regulatory body that has issued practise guidelines, known as the IPMA Recommendations, that members are expected to follow. Its specific interests are new issues, for example with the co-operation between underwriters in a syndicate, the timing of issues and the use of standard documentation for issues. Members of IPMA are required to belong to ISMA.

A breach of the IPMA's guidelines is not an offence because IPMA is a non-statutory body. However, the association operates very much on the lines of a traditional gentleman's club. The ultimate sanction is expulsion from the association, the consequences of which probably would be severe, IPMA members refusing to continue dealing with the expelled member, by not inviting the former member to join a syndicate.

The clearing and settlement of transactions in eurosecurities is arranged through one of the two international securities depositories, Clearstream and Euroclear that record ownership of the securities of their clients/members in electronic form. Transfers between buyer and seller are made within the system electronically, by book-entry transfer. There is no requirement for physical delivery of bonds from seller to buyer.

The settlement price for convertibles is calculated in a similar way to prices for eurobonds. The transaction price at which a trade is agreed is the clean price, exclusive of any accrued interest. The buyer pays on settlement a dirty price – the clean price plus accrued interest up to the settlement date.

Example
A 7.5% convertible bond pays interest semi-annually, on January 6 and July 6. A quantity of bonds is sold to an investor at a price of 96.50, for settlement on March 6.

Analysis
The clean price is 96.50, but the investor also must pay accrued interest on settlement. Accrued interest is for two months (January 6-March 6) and amounts to 1.25 per 100 face value of the bonds.

Clean price	96.50
Accrued interest	1.25
Dirty price, payable on settlement	97.75

The price at which the bond is traded is 96.50, but the price that the buyer will pay on settlement of the transaction is 97.75, to allow for the accrued interest.

Market Activity

The euroconvertibles market is much smaller than the eurobond and euroequities markets but market activity fluctuates as convertibles go in and out of fashion with issuers and investors.

Japanese Domestic Market

The Japanese domestic market is a large market for convertibles and although it can be accessed by foreign issuers, it has been used predominantly by Japanese companies for raising capital.

A typical issue is callable at any time from half-way to final maturity. For example, if a convertible is issued with a final maturity of ten years, the issuer typically will have the right to exercise a call option at any time from the end of the fifth year.

Summary

The convertible bond markets generally are smaller and less liquid than comparable bond and equity markets. There is a large domestic market in several countries, including the US and Japan. The euroconvertibles market has gone through periods of activity followed by inactivity, but remains fairly small.

Preferred Stock

Preferred stock are non-equity shares, although they are sometimes described incorrectly as equity.

Non-equity shares can be defined as shares that:

- give their holder entitlement to receive a dividend, but only up to a specific limit, and/or
- give their holder only a limited right to participate in any surplus in a winding up, should there be a liquidation and sale of the company's assets, and
- could be redeemable on fixed terms or on terms dictated by the issuer.

Dividend and Rights in a Liquidation

An annual preference dividend is payable, usually in two equal six-monthly amounts. This is a fixed percentage amount of the nominal value of the share. Unlike bond interest that is paid out of pre-tax profits, preference dividend comes out of post-tax profits. It must be paid before any dividend can be paid to equity (ordinary) shareholders.

In the liquidation of the company, preferred stockholders rank behind creditors and ahead of equity shareholders in the order of entitlement to payment from the proceeds of selling off the company's assets. The amount receivable in a winding up will be limited to the nominal value of the shares and possibly unpaid dividend.

Types of Preferred Stock

A straight or conventional preferred stock has the following characteristics:

- Interest is paid at a fixed annual rate, but only if profits are sufficiently high for the company to afford the dividend.
- When any due dividend is unpaid, the shareholders do not have the right to payment in arrears at a later date.
- The share is perpetual, i.e. irredeemable or permanent.

Most preferred stock are not conventional in type, but rather one or more of the following:

- cumulative
- participating
- redeemable
- convertible.

Stocks can be a combination of these types, for example cumulative redeemable stocks.

Cumulative Preferred Stocks

Cumulative preferred stocks entitle their holder to a fixed rate of dividend, and if any due dividend is unpaid, the arrears of dividend remain payable and accumulate. The preferred stockholders must receive their arrears of dividend before any ordinary dividend can be paid to equity shareholders.

Example

A company with 10 million 6% cumulative preferred stocks of $1 in issue did not pay any dividend last year to its preferred or ordinary shareholders. It would like to resume dividend payments in the current year beginning with an interim dividend.

Analysis

The company cannot pay an interim dividend in the current year to ordinary shareholders (equity) until it has paid the preferred stockholders' dividend of $900,000, as follows:

	$
Arrears of dividend last year (6% of $10 million)	600,000
Interim dividend, current year	300,000
	900,000

If the preferred stocks had been non-cumulative, their holders would not be entitled to the arrears of dividend, and in the current year they would be entitled only to the interim dividend of $300,000.

Participating Preferred Stocks

Participating preferred stocks have extra dividend rights. In addition to receiving a fixed dividend, holders of these stocks also participate in the company's surplus profits. This extra participating dividend usually is set at a specified percentage of the dividend paid on the ordinary shares.

Redeemable Preferred Stocks

Redeemable preferred stocks are shares that either will be redeemed at a specified future date, or could be redeemed at a specified future date, at the option of either the company or the stockholders. Stocks, like bonds, can be redeemed at par or at a premium to par value.

Convertible Preferred Stocks

Convertible preferred stocks give their holder the right to convert their stocks into ordinary shares of the company, at a specified future date or between specified future dates, at a specified rate of conversion. Convertible preferred stocks usually are redeemable; if they are not converted into equity, eventually they will be redeemed.

Convertible preferred stocks are similar in many respects to convertible bonds, although the method of quoting prices differs between:

- domestic markets, where preferred stocks are quoted in the same way as equity shares, and

- the international markets (euromarkets) where in a similar way to bonds, they are quoted as a percentage of par value.

Example 1
A multinational group might issue redeemable convertible preferred stocks in the euromarket. The issue might be made by its Netherlands Antilles-based finance subsidiary, backed by guarantee from the parent company. The preferred stocks would be convertible into equity shares of the parent company.

Although described as preferred stock, these securities would have most of the characteristics of convertible bonds and would be referred to as bonds by market analysts. Their prices will be quoted in the same way as bond prices, relative to a par value of 100, e.g. 129.25.

They might have a put option also. Holders of the stocks or bonds might have the right to redeem them at 130.22 five years after their issue and at a higher value, perhaps 180.64, ten years after their issue. They also might be callable, at the option of the issuing company. There will be a final date for redemption of the stock that might be 15 years after issue.

Convertible Capital Bonds
Convertible capital bonds are an example of the close similarities between convertible bonds and convertible preferred stock.

Convertible capital bonds were first issued in the euroconvertibles market in 1989. Convertible capital bonds can be converted into redeemable convertible preferred stock at the option of the issuer.

Preferred Stock Yields

Yields to investors on preferred stock usually are shown in one or more of the following ways:

- as a current yield
- as a redemption yield in the case of redeemable shares
- as a yield to put in the case of redeemable convertible preferred stock.

Current Yield

Current yield is the gross dividend yield as a percentage of the share's current market price. It is similar to the current yield on bonds.

When no withholding tax is deducted, and dividends are paid gross, the current yield is calculated as follows:

$$\text{Current yield} = \frac{\text{Coupon rate of dividend}}{\text{Market price}} \times 100\%$$

Example

A company has in issue 6.75% redeemable convertible preferred stock issued in the euroconvertibles market. The price of the stock is 132, i.e. 132% of face value.

In the euroconvertibles market, dividend is paid gross, without deduction of withholding tax. The current yield on the stock is:

$$\frac{6.75}{132} \times 100\% = 5.11\%$$

When tax is deducted at source from the dividend payment by the company, the current yield on the stock would be calculated as follows:

$$\text{Current yield} = \frac{(\text{Cash dividend} + \text{Tax deducted})}{\text{Market price}} \times 100\%$$

Redemption Yield

In the case of redeemable preferred stock, redemption yield is the average annual return to investors, based on the current share price, of dividends to the redemption date and the repayment of the capital on redemption. It is calculated in the same way as the redemption yield on bonds.

Yield to Put

Convertible redeemable preferred stock could give its holders a put option to redeem the shares early. In such cases, a yield to put can be calculated. This is similar to the yield to put for convertible bonds, i.e. it is a redemption yield, assuming that redemption will occur at the next put option exercise date.

Preferred Stock Markets

The markets for preferred stock are small, and contained within larger domestic and international markets.

In domestic markets, preferred stock is traded in the same way as equity shares and corporate bonds. Stock can be listed on a stock exchange and traded through the exchange dealing system. Domestic issues of preferred stock can be quite small, and it is usual to issue them as part of a company financial restructuring, or through a private placement to a small group of investors. Public issues of preferred stock are rare in all domestic stock markets.

In international markets, companies occasionally issue redeemable convertible preferred stock. These are regarded as part of the euroconvertibles market, together with convertible bonds and equity warrant bonds.

Auction Market Preferred Stock (Amps)

Auction market preferred stock (Amps) is a particular type of preferred stock. Its main distinguishing feature is that the dividend payable on the stock is determined by auction at regular intervals. A market for Amps exists in the US.

Amps are issued in the US through an investment bank or securities house that acts as a lead manager for the issue. They are sold to investors through the auction process. They cannot be offered for sale to the general public, and cannot be traded on a stock exchange.

A panel of investors is invited to participate in the auction. These investors submit bids for the dividend rate they will accept in return for buying a quantity of the stock. The stock is sold at a fixed price to the investors bidding the lowest dividend.

Example
A US company is issuing Amps, and a group of investment institutions is invited to bid for the stock. The size of the issue is $100 million. Bids are received for $60 million at a dividend yield of 6%, $90 million at a dividend yield of 6.25% and $150 million at a yield of 6.5%.

Analysis
The shares will be sold to the investors bidding the lowest dividend yield. However, the same dividend must be paid on all the stock. Because there is $100 million of stock for auction and only $80 million of bids at a dividend yield of 6%, the stock will be sold at a dividend yield of 6.25%.

Investors who bid 6% will receive the quantity of stock they asked for, ($60 million) and receive a dividend of 6.25%. The remaining $40 million stock will be sold to investors bidding for a 6.25% dividend.

The purchase price of the stock is its par value.

Subsequent Auctions
Auctions occur at regular intervals of at least every four weeks. Anyone wishing to buy Amps at an auction can submit a bid to receive a dividend yield of their choice. Bidders are existing holders of the stock and investors wishing to acquire some of the stock. The stock can change hands at each auction, i.e. a holder of stock could be required to sell at par to another bidder who submits a bid for a lower dividend yield.

At any subsequent auction after the primary issue, the existing holders of Amps can make any of the following three choices:

- *Hold.* An investor can decide to hold the Amps and agree to receive whatever rate of dividend is determined by the auction. Amps subject to hold orders are not available for sale.
- *Bid.* An investor can submit a bid to hold the Amps, but specify

the dividend yield required. The investor will retain the stock only if the dividend determined by auction is equal to or higher than the rate that he/she bid.

- *Sell.* An investor can try to sell the Amps at par to another bidder in the auction. To do this, he/she must submit a bid for a dividend yield that he/she expects to be higher than the successful bids in the auction. If an existing holder fails to submit a bid, he/she is deemed to have submitted a hold order.

When all orders have been received, an auction agent is responsible for deciding the allocation.

The number of Amps for which bid orders have been received is compared with the number of Amps available. If the volume of orders exceeds the number of Amps available, the dividend rate is set at the lowest rate at which all the Amps will be taken up. All holders will receive this same rate of dividend. Amps then must be sold by existing holders who bid a higher dividend rate to successful new buyers who bid a lower rate.

At each auction there is a maximum rate of dividend that will be paid on the stock. This depends on the credit rating of the stock at the time of the auction and is determined by a pre-set formula. If the credit rating of the stock is downgraded, the maximum rate payable is raised because stockholders should expect a bigger dividend when the credit risk increases. This rate of dividend is used as a default rate.

There could be insufficient bidders in an auction for the number of Amps available at a dividend below this maximum default rate. All the existing holders who want to sell will be unable to do so. The dividend rate payable until the next auction that must be a minimum of 28 days away, is the default rate.

Example
Alpha Inc, a US company, has an issue of $500 million of Amps. In an auction, bids are submitted for $300 million of stock at yields ranging from 4.5% to 5% and there were hold orders for $150 million. The maximum rate is 5%.

Analysis

There are insufficient bids for the stock. Bidders for $300 million will be able to buy the stock. Existing holders of $150 million of stock will retain their holding. Holders of a further $50 million of stock ($500m – $300m – $150m) who wanted to sell the stock will be unable to do so. They must hold their stock at least until the next auction. The dividend rate payable to the next auction is the default rate of 5%.

Interest Payments and Yields to Investors

Dividends on Amps are paid at pre-determined intervals and can be fairly frequent, matching the auction cycle.

Although they are called preferred stock, Amps are similar in many respects to bonds. The dividend on Amps might be 1% above the cost of straight short-term debt but the advantages are:

- there are no covenants attached to Amps issues, and
- they are redeemable only at the issuer's option.

The cost of Amps to the issuer will increase if the issuer's credit rating is downgraded. The default rate of dividend that applies if an auction is unsuccessful could be raised at the next auction.

Redemption of Amps

Amps are redeemable only at the option of the issuer, and in concept are perpetual. They are issued without covenants, and a failure to pay a due dividend does not constitute an event of default. Holders of shares cannot demand redemption when this happens.

However, Amps might not be perpetual finance. A company having issued Amps, could find that its credit rating has been downgraded so that the dividend payable will rise at subsequent auctions. If the credit rating is downgraded far enough, the cost of paying dividends on the Amps might become so high as to persuade the company to redeem them.

Percs

Percs are a proprietary product devised by Morgan Stanley, the US investment bank. Other investment banks and securities houses have devised similar products, such as Yield-Enhanced Securities (Yes) by Goldman Sachs that are used only in the US.

Percs are preferred equity redemption cumulative stock. They offer a higher dividend of about 30% more than common equity stock and must be redeemed at the end of three years. In effect, the investor is buying stock from the issuer and simultaneously selling the issuer a call option on the stock, the right to buy back at a predetermined price. However, the buy-back of Percs is in exchange for common equity. They are redeemed by issuing new equity shares rather than by a cash payment. Credit rating agencies in the US treat Percs as equity.

Percs

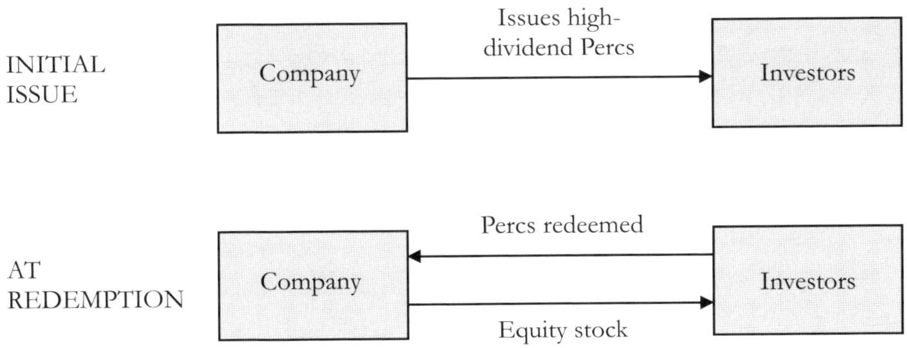

The terms of the redemption could be a one-for-one basis, the holder of Percs exchanging each unit of preferred stock for one ordinary share. A cap usually is placed on the potential benefit from a rising equity share price. If the ordinary share price has risen by more than a specified amount between the issue of the Percs and their redemption, the capital gain of the Percs investors is capped, and they receive less than one ordinary share for each unit of preferred stock.

Features of Percs are:

- a high dividend yield
- a redemption in exchange for common equity, and
- a cap on the capital gain.

Example
Beta Inc has issued $500 million of Percs with an 8% yield. The stock is redeemable three years after the issue date in exchange for equity shares of Beta. The rate of exchange is one equity share for each $50 of stock. The capital gain is capped at 30%. The current value of Beta's equity is $50.

Analysis
After three years, the Percs will be redeemed in exchange for 10 million equity shares in Beta ($500 million ÷ $50 per share) but only if the share price of Beta has risen by less than 30% in the time between issue and redemption, i.e. only if the share price is $65 or less.

If the share price on redemption were $80, the value of shares issued to the Percs holders would be capped at $650 million ($500 million on issue plus the 30% cap). Only 8,125,000 shares ($650m ÷ $80 per share) would be issued to redeem the Percs.

Summary

Preferred stock are non-equity shares with some characteristics similar to those of debt securities, particularly redeemable and convertible shares.

Innovations in the capital markets have included new forms of bonds and shares such as convertible capital bonds and Amps. These new types of security can be described as hybrid funding, neither equity nor debt, but containing features of both.

Equity Warrants

A share warrant is a certificate that gives its holder the right, but not the obligation, to purchase, at a fixed price:

- a number of equity shares of a company (equity warrants) or
- a quantity of bonds issued by a company (bond warrants).

Warrants are similar to call options on shares, and sometimes are referred to as options. A call option on shares gives its owner the right, but not the obligation, to purchase a quantity of shares on a specified future date or dates, or at any time between two dates, and at a specified price. Options that are issued by companies under employee share-option schemes are not marketable. However, share options issued by dealers are traded on stock exchanges or options exchanges. Warrants also are marketable, and can be exchange-traded.

The issuer of a warrant usually is the company whose shares or bonds can be purchased by the warrant holder. If the warrant rights are exercised, the warrant holder subscribes for shares or bonds in the company, and the company issues new shares or new bonds at the fixed price, known as the exercise price. Because warrants give their holder the right to subscribe for new shares or bonds, they also are known as subscription rights.

Warrants are valid for a specified period of time, after which they expire if unused. The right to exercise the warrant could be on specified future dates or at any time from a specified date up to expiry.

Warrants are described as American style if they can be exercised at any time up to expiry, and European style if they can be exercised only on a specific date. These terms are borrowed from the options market in which they are used more commonly.

Example
Alpha plc, a UK company, has 50 million shares of £1 each in issue, and the current market value per share is 400p. The company issues one million share warrants, entitling their holders to subscribe for new Alpha equity shares in five years' time at a price of 480p.

Analysis
In five years, if all the warrants are exercised, the company will issue one million new shares and raise capital of £4.8 million. If no further shares have been issued by Alpha, the total number of equity shares in issue will rise from 50 million to 51 million.

When are Warrants Issued?

Warrants are issued either in registered or bearer form, as a certificate or document, or in dematerialized electronic form with a recognized depository, such as Clearstream or Euroclear.

- Equity warrants can be issued to a company's employees, giving them the right to subscribe for shares in the company at a fixed price and at a future date. In this respect, equity warrants are similar to employee share options. A difference is that the warrants may be sold to employees whereas employee share options are granted without charge.
- By far the most usual method of issuing warrants is to issue unsecured bonds with equity share warrants attached. Sometimes these are described as issues of equity warrant bonds.

Equity warrant bonds are hybrid financial instruments because they combine features of both equity, the subscription rights given by the warrants, and debt.

Equity Warrant Bonds

In an issue of equity warrant bonds, warrants are issued to the investors who buy the bonds. The warrants are detachable and can be resold in secondary market trading separate from the bonds. Typically the bonds have a maturity of five to ten years, whereas the warrants usually are exercisable earlier, typically after three to five years.

Equity warrant bonds are a hybrid security because they have two component elements:

- unsecured bonds, usually with a fixed coupon, for a given maturity, and
- equity share warrants.

Buyers of the bonds in the primary issue are offered the income from a bond – and the rights of an unsecured bondholder – and also the opportunity to benefit from future increases in the company's share price.

Example
Beta plc, a UK company, is planning an issue of bonds with share warrants attached. The 5% bonds will have a maturity of ten years, and will be redeemable at par. One warrant will be attached to each £100 of bonds.

The share warrants give their holder the right to subscribe for four equity shares in Beta at a price of 160p. This right can be exercised at any time after five years from the issue date, but expires after ten years when the bond is redeemable. Beta's share price is 125p.

Analysis
Buyers of the bonds are being offered a fixed-rate bond and, in addition, the opportunity to benefit from any increase in Beta's share price above 160p in the next five to ten years.

Suppose, for example, that after five years the share price is 180p. Holders of warrants could subscribe for four shares for each warrant they hold at a price of 160p per share. Beta would issue new shares in exchange for each warrant that is exercised, and the warrant holders would make an immediate gain of 80p per warrant (180 – 160p per share, for four shares). The warrant holder would exercise the warrant and subscribe for four new shares at a cost of 640p that would have a market value of 720p.

Why Issue Warrants with Bonds?

The purpose of issuing warrants is to enhance the attraction to investors of the bond issue. The equity element provided by the warrants could persuade investors to subscribe for bonds that:

- are unsecured, and
- offer a lower coupon rate of interest than the company would have to pay for a straight bond issue.

Detaching the Warrants from the Bonds

After the primary issue of equity warrant bonds has been made, the warrants are detachable from the bonds and can be traded separately. A stock-exchange listing can be obtained for the warrants and the bonds separately. The bonds, with the warrants detached, would be listed as straight bonds.

Bonds often are held as long-term investments, whereas share warrants usually are held short-term. Warrant holders can hope to resell the warrants in the secondary market at a profit. When equity warrant bonds are issued, it is usual for the bonds to be fairly illiquid, with little secondary-market trading, and for the warrants to be actively traded securities in a liquid market.

Secondary-market trading in share warrants can take place before and during the exercise period, i.e. the period during which the right to exercise the warrants is permitted.

Exercise Price

The exercise price for a warrant is the fixed share price at which the warrant holder can subscribe for shares in the company. When the warrants are issued, the exercise price is above the current share price. It is assumed, as with convertible bonds, that the share price will rise in future to a higher value than the exercise price.

If the share price does not rise above the exercise price, the warrant rights will not be exercised and the warrants eventually will expire unused and worthless.

Altering the Exercise Price

When a company issues new shares in a rights issue at a price below the current market price, or issues convertible bonds or new warrants, the value of any existing warrants already in issue could be affected adversely. As a result it is usual to make a provision when warrants are issued for the possibility of a subsequent issue of shares or equity-linked securities. The terms on which the warrants are issued would include a formula for reducing the subscription price that warrant holders have to pay to buy shares in the company.

Example

Suppose that a Japanese company issues equity warrant 4.5% dollar bonds, giving warrant holders the right to subscribe for shares in the company at a price of ¥1,350. Eighteen months later the company makes an issue of convertible bonds and two months after that, a further issue of equity warrant bonds. The terms of the 4.5% dollar bond issue should provide for the subscription price for these warrants to be reduced in these circumstances because the subsequent issue of convertibles and the further issue of equity warrant bonds is likely to affect the value of the company's shares. This is because of the larger potential dilution of equity. The exercise price for the warrants might be reduced from ¥1,350 to ¥1,340.

Equity Warrant Bonds: Option to Convert the Bonds into Shares

An issue of bonds with share warrants can include an option to convert the bonds into shares. The warrants would be exercised either by subscribing for shares in cash or by surrendering bonds.

Example
A company might issue ten-year 5.75% guaranteed bonds in Year 1 with 37,200 share warrants attached. Each share warrant might entitle the holder to subscribe for 866 equity shares in the period to March Year 11. The exercise price might be $3,968.90 per warrant (458.3¢ per share) until 20 March Year 3, rising in annual increments to $5,143.75 per warrant (594¢ per share) from 20 March Year 10. Alternatively, if the warrants have not been detached from the bonds, the terms of the issue might provide for a warrant to be exercised by surrendering one 5.75% guaranteed bond with a principal amount of $5,000, rather than by making a cash payment. The holder of the warrant and bond loses the bond, but is not required to pay any further money to acquire the shares.

The Value of Warrants

Warrants have a value. If they are listed on a stock exchange, their value is evident in the market price at which they are traded. However, it is useful to look at the basic principles of warrant pricing, and the concepts involved.

During the period in which a warrant can be exercised, its price should not fall below the higher amount of:

- a nil value, and
- the amount by which the current share price exceeds the exercise price, multiplied by the number of shares obtainable from each warrant. This is known as the *theoretical value* of the warrant.

Theoretical value = (Current share price – Exercise price) x Number of shares per warrant.

For example, if a share warrant entitles its holder to subscribe for one share in a company at 170¢ and the current share price is 210¢, the theoretical value of the warrant is 40¢. In principle, but not necessarily in practise, the warrant's market price should be 40¢ or higher.

When the warrants are issued, and in secondary-market trading before expiry, they can have a market value, even when the current share price is below the exercise price. The value of equity warrants is similar in concept to the conversion premium for convertible bonds. It is a value that arises from the possibility that the share price will rise above the exercise price before the warrants expire. This value is the amount that investors should be prepared to pay to buy the warrants.

How are Warrants Priced?

The market, dealers and investors, has to put a value on share warrants in order to trade in them. The method of valuation for share warrants is similar in concept to the method of valuation for options. A number of pricing models have been developed for options and warrants, based on adaptations of a formula known as the Black-Scholes model after its creators. The pricing model is complex and beyond the scope of this book.

In concept the market value of a warrant is:

- its theoretical value, if any, plus
- a premium for the option to subscribe for shares in the future at a fixed price, a subscription premium or conversion premium.

The exercise price could be higher than the share's current market price, and the warrant could be said to have a negative theoretical value. Its market price would then be the value of the premium for the subscription rights minus the negative theoretical value.

Warrant Pricing

Theoretical value (positive or negative)	+	Premium for subscription rights	=	Value of warrant

Warrant Conversion Premium

In secondary-market trading the current price of the warrant is known, so the warrant's conversion premium can be calculated as:

- the amount by which the exercise price plus the warrant's market price together exceed the current share price
- multiplied by the number of shares that the warrant entitles its holder to buy.

Example

An investor holds equity warrants that can be used to subscribe for ordinary shares in Gamma Inc on a one-for-one basis at an exercise price of 250¢. The current share price is 225¢ and the warrants are quoted on the market at 50¢.

There is a warrant premium, calculated as follows:

	cents	**cents**
Cost (market price) of warrant		50
Exercise price	310	
Current share price	300	
Amount by which exercise price exceeds current share price	10	
Number of shares per warrant	1	
Excess x Number of shares (10 x 1)		10
Warrant premium		60

This calculation could be shown in a slightly different way. The market price of a warrant is its theoretical value plus a premium. The theoretical value is negative when the exercise price exceeds the current share price. In this example:

	cents	cents
Market price of warrant		50
Current share price	300	
Exercise price	310	
Theoretical value	– 10	
Number of shares per warrant	1	
Theoretical value x Number of shares		
(Negative, so add)		+ 10
Warrant premium		60

The premium can be expressed as a percentage of the current share price. In this example, it would be 20% (60 ÷ 300 x 100%).

In the short term, the market price of a warrant tends to move more or less in line with movements in the share price. If the share price rises 5¢, the warrant's price is likely to rise by about the same amount.

Example

Returning to the example above, suppose that the share price rises from 300¢ to 355¢. The market price of a warrant also could rise by 55¢, to 105¢ giving the warrant holder a profit of 55¢ per warrant – 110% profit on the initial investment.

In the example above, the warrant could be used to subscribe for one share. The same calculation could be made when a warrant could be used to subscribe for any other number of shares. For example, suppose that a warrant could be used to subscribe for five shares in a company, at an exercise price of 500¢, that the current share price is 480¢ and the market value of the warrant is 60¢.

The value of the premium (subscription rights) would be calculated as:

	cents	cents
Cost (market price) of warrant		60
Exercise price	500	
Current share price	480	
Amount by which exercise price exceeds current share price	20	
Number of shares per warrant	5	
Excess x Number of shares (10 x 3)		100
Warrant premium		160

The premium would be 160¢ per warrant, or 32¢ per share (five shares per warrant).

Factors Influencing the Size of a Warrant Premium

In the long term the price of the warrant and hence the premium will depend on:

- the length of time before the warrants may be exercised
- the current price of shares compared to the exercise price, and
- the future prospects of the company.

As the exercise period approaches, the premium will disappear. During the exercise period there should be no premium because, if there were, it would be cheaper to buy the shares directly rather than buy the warrant to subscribe for shares. During the exercise period for the warrant, the market value of the warrant should be its theoretical value (see above) or, if the exercise price is higher than the current share price, nil.

In-the-Money and Out-of-the-Money Warrants

When the current share price exceeds the warrant's exercise price, the intrinsic value or theoretical value is positive. The warrant can be described as in-the-money, using terms more commonly applied to share options.

When the exercise price is higher than the current share price, the warrant has no intrinsic value. Its theoretical value is negative, but no security can have a negative market price. The warrant will not be exercised unless the share price rises. The warrant could retain a market value, but it could be described as out-of-the-money, again using terminology more commonly applied to share options.

Parity

Warrants trade at parity when the warrant price plus the exercise price equals the current share price, i.e. when the premium is zero.

Occasionally a warrant can trade at a discount to parity. The share's market price will be higher than the exercise price plus the warrant's market price. This can happen when:

- the warrant is not American-style and exercisable at any time, but can be exercised only on certain specific dates or between two dates in the future, and
- the market expects the share price to fall before the first exercise date, perhaps because a large dividend payment is imminent.

Warrants and Share-Price Speculation

Warrants are bought mainly as short-term investments with a view to reselling them at a profit. An investor wishing to speculate on an increase in a company's share price can purchase warrants rather than shares. The total cost of the speculative investment in warrants would be less than the cost of an investment in shares. This is because the warrants have a much lower market value than shares.

- If the share price falls in value, the warrant's price also will fall, possibly to zero. The investor could lose the full cost of the investment.
- If the share price rises, the warrant's price also should increase. The profit to the warrant holder, in percentage terms, should be much greater than the profit that would have been obtained by purchasing shares. This is because the price of the warrants will

tend to move more or less in line with the price of the share. Thus, if the share price rises by 50¢ the increase in the value of the warrant will be about the same.

Example

Delta Inc has issued share warrants. Each warrant gives its holder the right to subscribe for one Delta equity share at a price of 290¢. The current share price is 270¢ and the market price of a warrant is 30¢.

An investor expects Delta's share price to rise, and is considering the purchase or either 100,000 Delta shares or 100,000 Delta share warrants.

Analysis

The shares would cost $270,000 to buy, and the warrants would cost just $30,000.

If the share price went up by 10¢ to 280¢, the value of the warrant could rise by a similar amount, to 40¢.

The investor could have made a profit of $10,000 or 3.7% (10 ÷ 30 x 100%) by purchasing shares, and a profit of $10,000 or 33.3% (10 ÷ 30 x 100%) by purchasing warrants.

The high ratio of increase, or decrease, in profits per $1 invested in warrants is referred to as a high-gearing effect. A relatively small change in the share price can result in a relatively large percentage increase in the profit or loss on an investment in warrants.

Gearing for warrants can be measured as the share price divided by the market value of the warrant. This can be used as a measure of the profit potential from investing in the warrants. The ratio of share price to warrant price, or gearing, normally should be at least four times to justify investing in the warrants.

Price Volatility

Because warrants often involve a high degree of gearing, a relatively small movement in the share price results in a disproportionately large movement in the price of the warrant making the prices of warrants extremely volatile.

Advantages of Warrants

The advantages of equity warrants to a company are that:

- there is no payment of interest or dividends on warrants
- when issued with bonds, the coupon interest rate on the bonds can be lower than for a straight bond issue
- the company can establish a means of increasing its equity funds at a future date without any immediate dilution of profits per share. In contrast, a rights issue at an issue price below the share's current market value often has the effect in the short term of reducing the company's earnings per share.

For investors, the benefits of warrants are low downside risk and the potential for large profits should the share price rise.

Risks with Warrant Issues

The main risk with an issue of equity warrant bonds, for both the issuer and the investor, is that the share price could fall, rather than rise.

- The warrants will expire worthless if their exercise price is higher than the market price for the shares. The warrant investors would lose their investment. The bond investors also might be affected because if the credit status of the company has declined, the credit rating for the bond issue might be downgraded. If the credit rating is downgraded, the market price of the bond will fall, to reflect the higher official credit risk.
- A company seeking to raise new funds as its old bond issue expires will be regarded as much more of a credit risk by the investment community, and as a consequence probably will have to pay higher interest rates in the future on any new bond issue.

The Market for Share Warrants
The market for share warrants is not large, although particular types of company issue them regularly, for example investment companies in the UK. However, there is active trading in some warrant issues.

Equity Warrant Bonds and Convertible Bonds Compared

Equity warrant bonds and convertible bonds are hybrid instruments. In the international bond markets, companies issue bonds in both forms. It is helpful to look at the relative merits and uses of each type of hybrid, with particular reference to:

- raising finance
- their market valuation and the price at which they can be issued
- investors in each type of hybrid
- call flexibility
- the combination of swaps with bond issues
- maturity.

Raising finance
When a company issues convertible bonds, it obtains all the finance up front when the bonds are issued. For equity warrant bonds, the company raises finance for the bonds when they are issued, but will not raise finance from the warrants until later, when the warrants are exercised.

Valuation
As indicated earlier, theoretical value for a share warrant can be calculated from the same type of pricing model that is used to value share options (the Black-Scholes model). In practise, however, investors usually are willing to pay only a fraction of what a warrant should be worth in theory. Investors will pay more for the conversion premium on an issue of convertibles than they will pay for the warrants in an issue of

equity warrant bonds. It is often the case that a company could raise more capital by issuing convertible bonds than by issuing bonds with warrants attached.

Investor Base

Although warrants can have a long term to expiry, often they are held by short-term investors who buy warrants in the expectation of reselling them at a profit when the company's share price rises. Until the exercise date for the warrant is approaching, they do not intend to hold the warrants in order to subscribe for equity shares in the future.

This is in contrast to investors in convertible bonds who are much more likely to hold their bonds until conversion into equity or redemption.

Call Flexibility

Bonds with warrants usually are non-callable. The company cannot force warrant holders into an immediate decision about whether or not to subscribe for equity shares.

Swaps

An advantage of equity warrant bond issues over convertible bond issues is the ability to arrange a swap without risk.

Example

A Japanese company wishes to raise capital in yen, but sees a favorable opportunity for an issue of dollar bonds in the international market. The company believes it must offer investors either a convertible bond issue or a bond issue with share warrants attached.

Analysis

The company is issuing bonds in dollars, but wants to convert them into yen. To avoid an exposure to currency risk, it should try to convert its dollar liabilities, the payments on the bonds, into yen liabilities. This can be arranged through a currency swap with a bank specializing in swap transactions.

In a currency swap, the company can arrange to exchange:

- regular interest payments. In this example, the company can pay the bank in yen at a fixed rate and receive in exchange payments in dollars, also at a fixed interest rate
- yen for dollars at maturity of the swap, at a fixed rate of exchange.

The company will issue dollar bonds and convert the dollars into yen. Through the swap arrangement, it pays interest and principal at maturity to the swaps bank in yen, and receives interest and principal from the swaps bank in dollars. The dollar inflows can be arranged so as to match the company's liability to pay interest and debt principal at maturity to its bondholders.

Currency Swap

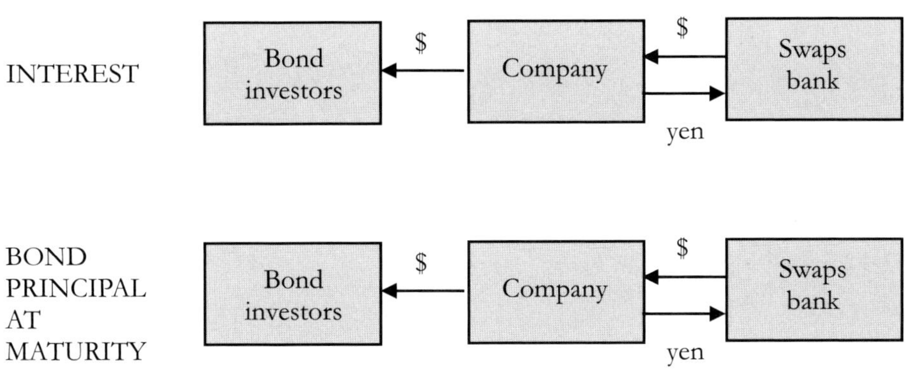

For a swap to meet the requirement to avoid currency risk, the company has to be certain that interest payments on the bonds will be made until a fixed date such as maturity, and at this fixed date the bonds will be redeemed at a known cost. The maturity of the swap can be made to coincide with redemption of the bonds.

If the company issues bonds with warrants attached, redemption is certain. If the warrants are exercised, this does not affect the company's obligation to redeem the bonds.

In contrast, if the company issues convertibles, it cannot be sure the bonds will be redeemed or whether they will be converted into equity.

If a company intends to convert the proceeds of an equity-linked bond issue into a different currency it might prefer to issue bonds with warrants rather than convertibles.

Maturity

The maturity of a bond issued with share warrants attached is predictable. The bond portion remains outstanding until maturity.

In contrast, a convertible bond could remain outstanding for a much shorter time, and be either converted into equity or redeemed through a put or call option long before final maturity.

If a company requires certainty of redemption dates for its financial planning, equity warrant bonds would be preferable to conventional convertibles.

Bonds with Debt Warrants

Very occasionally, bonds are issued with debt warrants attached. These are warrants that give their holder the right to subscribe for new bonds or other debt securities in the company, at a fixed price. For example, an issue of 10% bonds could be made with warrants that give their holders the right to subscribe at a future date for more 10% bonds, at a fixed price.

Investors who expect interest rates on bonds to fall at a future date could be attracted by these warrants. A fall in interest rates would make the warrants more valuable because they offer the right to subscribe for bonds offering a coupon rate that is now relatively high.

Covered Warrants

Covered warrants differ from ordinary warrants in two significant ways.

- They are issued by a securities house rather than by the company from whom shares can be subscribed with the warrants. The aim of the securities house is to create an active and liquid market in the warrants and to earn profits from making a market in them.
- When ordinary warrants are exercised, the holder applies to the company to subscribe for new shares. In contrast, for covered warrants, the securities house cannot issue new shares in the company concerned. When covered warrants are exercised, there is no recourse to the company, and the company does not issue new shares. The securities house must settle the warrant holder's application to subscribe for shares, either by providing shares already in issue or by the payment of sufficient cash to allow the current holder to buy the shares in the market.

Summary

An equity warrant issued by a company gives its holder the right to subscribe for a quantity of shares in a company at a predetermined price – the exercise price – on any one of a number of specified future dates, or at any time between two specified dates. A warrant in effect is a long-dated call option on shares issued by the company.

Most warrants are issued in a package with bonds, in both domestic and international bond markets. Issues are less frequent that conventional straight bond issues. After issue, warrants can be detached from the bonds and traded separately.

Warrants have a theoretical minimum value, or intrinsic value, but often trade at a premium to this value, similar to the conversion premium on convertible bonds. The size of this premium depends on the remaining life to expiry of the warrant, the exercise price relative to the share price, and share-price volatility or growth expectations. Warrants can produce high returns on a relatively small investment for investors wishing to speculate on a share-price increase.

Equity warrant bonds offer an alternative to convertible bonds as a form of hybrid security. The relative popularity of each type can vary over time. At present there are a greater number of convertible bond issues than equity warrant bond issues.

Mezzanine Finance

In the chapters so far, hybrid instruments have been described largely in terms of large public companies and stock markets. Hybrids, however, are often a feature of corporate financing arrangements agreed privately between a company's management and a small group of investors. Convertible bonds or preferred stock, for example, could be issued as part of a refinancing agreement (a rescue package) between a struggling company and its creditors. Another common use of hybrids is to provide mezzanine finance for the purchase of a company, often by its management.

The term mezzanine finance can be used to describe any funding that lies between senior debt and equity in the ranking for payment in the event of the company's liquidation. It could include, for example, preferred stock capital.

Management Buy-outs and Buy-ins

A management buyout or MBO is the purchase of a company from its existing shareholders by a team comprising the company's managers. A management buy-in or MBI is the purchase of a company by an incoming new management team.

Financing an MBO or MBI

To raise finance for a buy-out, the managers involved will be expected to provide some equity capital themselves. However, usually they will rely for most of the financing on venture-capital organizations and banks. This finance, when forthcoming, usually is provided as a mixture of equity capital, senior debt finance and mezzanine finance.

Senior debt is fully secured bank lending that ranks first among creditors for repayment in the event of liquidation of the company. It can consist of term loans, revolving facilities and overdrafts.

Mezzanine finance normally is also secured lending, but ranks after senior debt but ahead of the equity in the event of a liquidation of the company. To compensate the lender for the higher credit risk, the interest rate payable on mezzanine finance is higher than on senior debt. In addition, the lender might receive an incentive or kicker, usually equity-linked.

An equity kicker is a share option or warrant given to a mezzanine loan provider to acquire equity in the company. This is intended to act as a further incentive to a lender to provide mezzanine finance rather than to insist on senior debt lending, or refuse to lend at all.

A kicker might not take the form of share warrants or options. A warrant is most appropriate when the lender expects the company to succeed, so that its share value will rise substantially. Non-equity kickers include a premium on the redemption of the loan or a back-end loan fee, i.e. a fee paid on redemption.

MBO Funding Mix

MBOs and MBIs usually are financed by debt capital and are a form of highly leveraged transaction (HLT). A highly leveraged transaction can be defined as a company-purchase arrangement that creates a highly leveraged financing structure – high debt to equity ratio – for the company.

The mix of equity, senior debt and mezzanine finance varies with each MBO, conditions in the debt markets, and the perceived risks of excessive borrowing and high gearing.

The possible funding mix, according to market conditions, might be either of the following.

	Equity	Mezzanine Finance	Senior Debt
When high gearing is discouraged	c40%- 45%	c5% - 10%	c 45% - 55%
When high gearing is more acceptable to lenders	c25%	c10%	c65%

Geared financing is risky for the company because it could be forced into liquidation if it cannot meet its loan obligations. However, geared finance is necessary if equity shareholders are to expect a very high return on their own investment that often is a precondition of their willingness to put equity finance into the MBO. Mezzanine finance can help the MBO team to achieve a suitable balance between equity and debt in the buyout funding arrangement.

Risks and Cost of MBO Finance

The cost of the senior-debt capital for an MBO depends on conditions in the bank-lending market, and the bank's assessment of the credit risk of the borrower.

Providers of senior debt generally are risk-averse, and will want their lending to be fully secured without any prior rights for other creditors.

Institutional providers of equity take a bigger investment risk in the company because their investment is not secured. They recognize that if the company is not successful after its MBO, returns to equity shareholders could be low, and at worst they could lose their entire investment. Consequently, to compensate them for the high risk, they will expect the business plan for the MBO to promise a very high return.

A provider of mezzanine debt takes a middle view on risk, between the senior loan provider and the equity investor, and usually invests on the strength of the expected cash flows of the business.

Mezzanine finance usually is longer term than senior debt, typically five to ten years. In addition to receiving an equity kicker, the lender will expect a higher margin above LIBOR than the providers of senior-debt capital. The combination of the interest yield on the mezzanine debt and the expected returns from the equity kicker should offer a promised return in total somewhere between the interest rate on the senior debt and the yield expected by institutional investors in the company's equity.

Exit Route

It is usual for venture-capital organizations providing equity capital to seek an exit route from the MBO company after several years. An exit route provides venture capitalists with a means of selling their shares for cash to recover their investment and realize a profit. This could be achieved, for example, if the eventually company seeks a stock-exchange listing, or a trade sale of its business to another company. It is usual for providers of mezzanine loans to exercise their options or warrants, i.e. their equity kicker, at the same time, and take the same exit route as the equity shareholders.

Alternatively, because mezzanine finance is more expensive than senior debt, after a successful MBO, companies could try a few years, to negotiate a funding switch from mezzanine finance to senior debt by offering better security on the loan capital.

Key Characteristics of Mezzanine Finance

The key characteristics of mezzanine finance can be summarized as follows:

- Mezzanine finance is subordinate to senior debt, but gives the lender a higher interest yield.
- The subordination is determined by a deed of priority in UK agreements.
- An equity kicker usually is given to the lender in the form of share options or share warrants.
- The yield required depends on market conditions and investors' perception of the risk. The total yield is the interest on the loan plus the profits from the equity kicker.
- Mezzanine finance could make up about 10% of the total financing of an MBO, although the exact proportion varies with individual cases.
- Lenders will require various covenants from the company. Financial covenants are likely to include a minimum-interest-cover requirement. Lenders also will expect the company to have good cash flows from its trading operations.

Summary

Although mezzanine finance is most commonly associated with MBOs for medium-sized or small companies, it can be used for larger companies and in company refinancings, management buy-ins and acquisitions for which the buyer relies heavily on debt funding (leveraged acquisitions).

Asset-Backed Securities

What is Asset Securitization?

Asset-backed securities are not properly hybrid securities. They are securities, mainly bonds or notes, that are created by packaging together a collection of assets that will produce a future income. Bonds or notes are then issued, and the interest payments and loan principal repayment at maturity are paid for out of the income from the assets.

The assets must be capable of producing cash income. The assets should have good credit quality so that the risk of failing to earn the expected income is low. The total income from the package of assets taken as a whole must be predictable and reliable.

A company or institution that has assets that will generate future income can offer to sell the income on to investors.

- The company may have a low credit standing, even though its assets have a good credit quality. Investors might be more willing to invest in the company's assets than in the company.

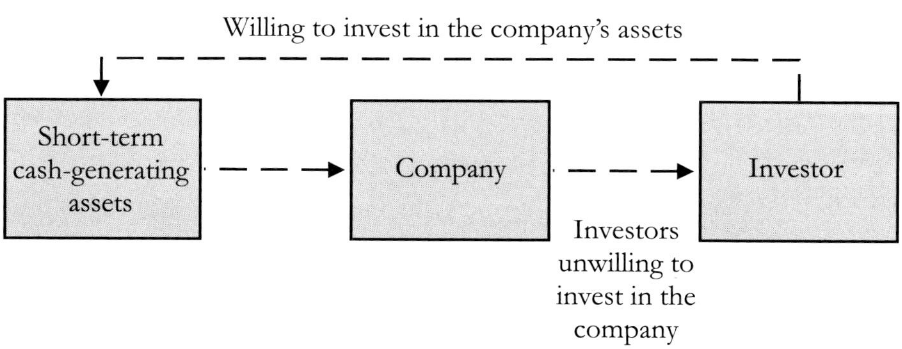

- An organization's assets could be expected to generate income over a long period of time. Mortgage loans, for example, could generate cash payments over many years. Many mortgage loans also have a good credit quality because the underlying property provides security for the loan. If an organization wishes to raise finance, it could offer to sell future income from its long-term assets to investors willing to invest in those assets.

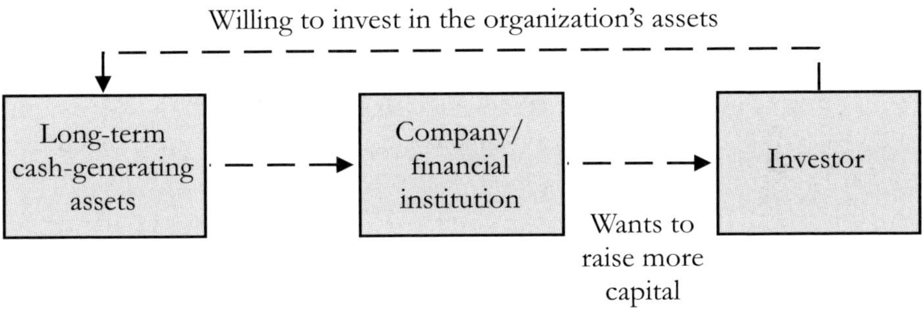

Example
Alpha Bank has made mortgage loans to a large number of customers, repayable in ten years' time. The total amount of mortgage loans is $1,000 million. The bank wishes to reduce its mortgage loan book by this amount.

It can do this by creating new ten-year bonds. If the credit risk were zero (that will not be the case in practise) the bank can create $1,000,000 of bonds and sell them to investors. Interest on the loans would continue to be collected by the bank that will take an agency fee for this service, but most of the interest received from the loans would be used to pay interest on the bonds.

The bonds are backed by the mortgage loans of the bank that are assets of the bank. It could be said that the rights to the mortgage loan income have been turned into bond securities, i.e. the mortgage loans have been securitized.

Origins

Asset securitization began in the US in the 1970s with mortgage-backed securities. Initially these were mortgages packaged together and guaranteed by one of the government mortgage agencies, the Government National Mortgage Association or GNMA (Ginnie Mae), the Federal Home Loan Mortgage Association or FHLMA (Freddie Mac) or the Federal National Mortgage Association or FNMA (Fannie Mae). The market for asset-backed securities in Europe began somewhat later.

The market has since expanded considerably, and a wide range of revenue-earning assets might be securitized including car loans and credit-card receivables.

Special-Purpose Vehicles (SPVs)

The method of establishing an asset securitization programme is for an organization, such as a financial intermediary, to set up an off-balance sheet organization, referred to in general terms as a special purpose vehicle or SPV, or as a conduit vehicle. This is a specially created company, perhaps with a sequence number in its name, such as Mortgage Funding Corporation Number 6 Inc. or Mortgage Funding Corporation Number 7 Inc.

The SPV purchases cash-generating assets from either one or a number of different sellers. The assets are packaged together, and the SPV issues bonds or notes backed by the package of assets. The proceeds from selling the bonds are used to pay the asset owner for the right to the assets. For example, if a bank is securitizing some mortgage loans, the SPV will pay the bank for the loans it purchases out of the income from issuing the bonds.

Any security or guarantees attached to the assets are transferred from the seller of the assets to the SPV.

The sale of assets to the SPV is without recourse. This means that the seller receives an agreed price for the assets, and will not be required to make up any shortfall should the level of bad debts/non-payment exceed actuarial forecasts. The credit risk from the assets is taken on by the SPV that must bear any losses from non-payment and debt write-off.

Establishing and Operating the SPV

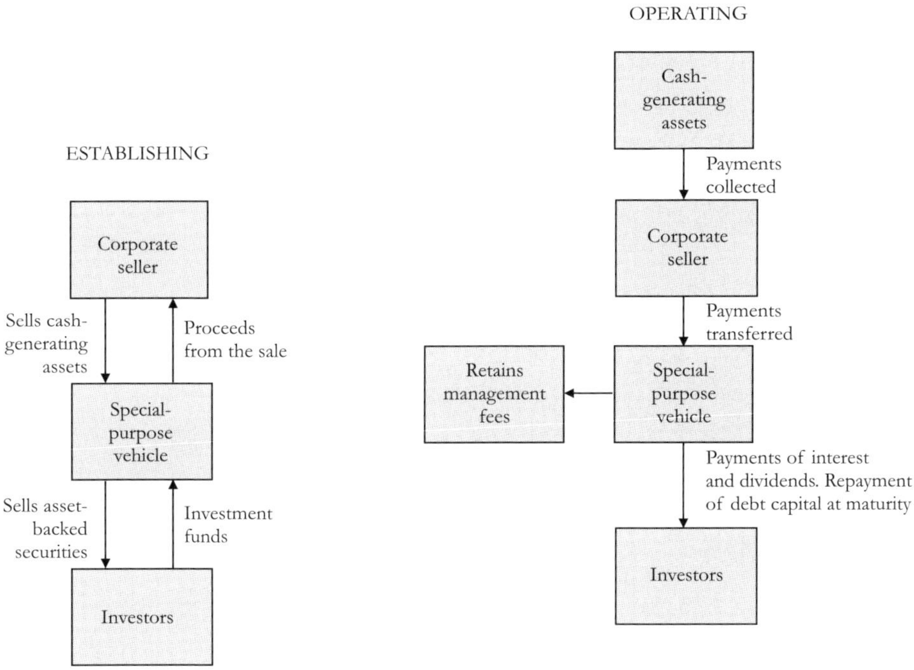

Credit Quality

For asset-backed securities to attract investors, they must have a sufficiently high credit quality. This could be provided by the credit quality of the underlying assets. However, normally there is some credit risk, even with high-quality assets. Investors in asset-backed securities must be offered some form of cushion against the risk of default by the SPV, i.e the risk of failure to pay loan interest on the bonds, or redeem the loan principal at maturity.

There are several ways in which this can be done, and more than one of these methods can be used in combination if required. Three methods are:

- over-collateralization
- a tiered capital structure
- credit enhancement.

Over-Collateralization

The value of the assets of the SPV could exceed the funding liabilities, that is the amount of bonds or notes issued. For example, mortgage loans for $1,000 million could be packaged by an SPV and $950 million of bonds issued, backed by these loans. This would allow for a bad debt rate of 5% ($50 million) on the loans.

Tiered Capital Structure

The SPV could issue two or more different classes of security, such as senior debt, subordinated debt and equity securities. Each class of security would have a different credit risk. A higher return would be offered to the investors in the higher-risk classes of security, but they would be entitled to their income only after investors in the lower-risk classes are paid what they are owed.

Example

A bank wishes to set up a special-purpose vehicle and securitize some of its mortgage loan portfolio. For every $100 of loans the SPV that is used issues $95 of bonds and sells these bonds to investors. Investors in these bonds will receive interest at a specified rate. The SPV also issues $5 of subordinated debt for each $100 of mortgage loans in the package, and issues this perhaps to the bank itself. The holder of the subordinated loans will receive the residual income from the mortgage loans after the senior bondholders have received what they are owed and after the payment of management fees/commissions to the SPV.

Credit Enhancement

The SPV might arrange for a third-party organization to provide a guarantee. Alternatively, the SPV might purchase credit insurance from a specialist insurance provider to guarantee payment to the SPV bond investors in the event that the SPV is unable to meet its obligations on the bonds. The bonds of the SPV would then have the same credit rating as the guarantor. This type of arrangement is known as credit enhancement.

Asset-backed securities are given a credit rating by one of the credit rating agencies such as Moody's and Standard & Poor's.

Issuing Asset-Backed Securities

Asset securitization can be arranged on behalf of an organization by a financial intermediary such as a bank.

- The bank can discuss an arrangement with an individual company that has cash-generating assets it might wish to sell. However, the value of the company's cash-generating assets must be sufficiently large to justify a stand-alone deal.
- The bank may invite a number of companies to discuss a common deal to sell selected cash-generating assets.
- A bank might wish to sell some of its own assets, such as mortgage loans.

The bank will investigate the assets of the potential clients to decide whether or not they are suitable for securitization. The bank also will ask for information to assess the payments records of the client's debtors in order to predict the probable volume of bad debts. An agreement will be reached for the sale of selected assets by the client company, or the bank itself, to an SPV that is established for the purpose.

The SPV raises funds to purchase the assets by issuing securities that could be shares, bonds or commercial paper. Bonds or notes could offer either a fixed rate of interest or, more probably in the case of mortgage-backed securities, variable-rate interest.

There could be at least two classes of share or bond.

- Most securities will be in a class entitled to regular payments of interest or dividends out of the cash income generated by the assets. This class of bondholder or shareholder would be entitled to payment ahead of the holders of the other class of securities.
- A small proportion of securities will be in a higher-risk class. These would carry an entitlement to all the remaining income from the assets after payment of management charges to the SPV and the payment of interest or dividends to other classes of security.

The income from the assets is collected by the company that sold them to the SPV, and is paid over to the SPV. The SPV in turn uses this income to pay its security holders and its own charges/commissions.

Once the arrangement has been established, the company or bank selling the package of assets to the SPV will report regularly, typically monthly, on cash receipts from the assets, and on the current value of the assets that have been sold to the SPV and for which future payments are still receivable.

Example
Banque Beta, a French bank, set up a special-purpose vehicle (known as an FCC in France) to purchase a selection of personal loans on which borrowers pay interest monthly. The average return on personal loans is 12% per annum. The FCC issues two classes of share.

- A shares that represent 92% of the nominal value of the personal loans purchased. The holders of A shares receive monthly payments at a rate of 7% per annum on the nominal value of the loans, plus any early repayments of loans received during the month.
- B shares that represent 8% of the nominal value of the personal loans purchased. The holders of the B shares receive all the remaining cash flows from the personal loans after

payment to the A shareholders and payment of management charges to the FCC.

The A shares, but not the B shares, are given a credit rating by two credit-rating agencies, and sold to investors.

Accounting Issues

Hybrid instruments combine features of both equity and debt. Because the financial reports of companies make a distinction between share capital and debt in the balance sheet, it might be useful to consider briefly how hybrids are treated in financial accounts.

Accounting for convertible bonds

Convertible bonds might be converted into equity shares of the company at some time in the future. If they are not converted, they will be redeemed. For balance-sheet reporting, the conversion of the bonds into equity is not anticipated, and it is assumed, until conversion takes place, that the bonds will be redeemed rather than converted. Consequently, convertible bonds are treated as a liability (debt payable) in the balance sheet of the company.

Accounting for the Conversion of Bonds

When convertible bonds are converted into equity shares of the company, the transaction is accounted for so that no profit or loss arises. The liability disappears from the balance sheet, and is replaced by share capital and reserves – an addition to the share premium account.

Example

A company has $2 million of convertible bonds in issue that are shown in the balance sheet as a liability at the face value of the debt. Each $100 of bonds can be converted into 25 equity shares of $1 each at any time three years after their issue.

Suppose that all the bonds are converted into equity shares after three years. The effect in the accounts will be as follows.

	Remove from balance sheet $	Add to balance sheet $
Convertible bonds (liability)	2,000,000	
Share capital (500,000 shares of $1)		500,000
Reserves (share premium): the balance		1,500,000
	2,000,000	2,000,000

Finance Costs

Convertible bonds usually are redeemed at par, but they may be redeemed at a premium to their par value. When they are redeemable at a premium, for example, if there is a put option, the premium is treated in the accounts as a finance cost. This cost must be provided for over the life of the bonds.

Convertibles usually are issued with a lower coupon than straight bonds. Some issues give their holders the option at some time in the future to give up their conversion rights so that the bonds become straight bonds. In return, the bondholders will receive either a premium on the redemption of the bonds, or supplemental interest. This is a payment of interest on the difference between the coupon on the convertibles and the coupon that would have been payable on straight bonds. Supplemental interest would be backdated to the date of issue of the bonds. Where supplemental interest, or a premium, is paid in these circumstances, they would be treated as a finance cost and charged against profits over the life of the bond.

An example showing the treatment of finance costs is shown at the end of this chapter.

Accounting for Warrants

When warrants are issued by a company, they are given a value and shown in the balance sheet of the company. They are treated as equity share capital, non-equity share capital or debt capital, depending on whether they can be used to subscribe for new equity shares, new preferred stock or new debt of the company.

When bonds are issued with equity warrants attached, the bonds are separated from the warrants for the purpose of balance-sheet reporting. If the bonds are issued at par value, this means they will be shown in the balance sheet at a discount to par value.

Example
A company issues $10 million of 5% bonds with equity warrants attached. They are issued at par. A valuation model is used to give a value of $500,000 to the warrants. In the balance sheet of the company, the warrants would be shown within share capital and reserves, probably as a special equity reserve, of $500,000, and the bonds would be shown with a value of $9,500,000, at a discount to par.

Accounting for the Exercise of Warrants
When warrants are exercised, the transaction is recorded in the accounts of the company so that no profit and no loss arises on the transaction. The valuation of the warrants in the balance sheet is removed, and transferred to share capital or reserves (share premium account).

Example
A company has a reserve in its balance sheet for equity warrants, valued at $500,000. All the warrants are exercised, and their holders subscribe for 200,000 new ordinary shares of $1 each in the company. The subscription price is $6 per share.

As a result of these transactions, the reserve account for the warrants will disappear, but there will be an addition to share capital of $200,000, and an addition to the share premium account of $1,000,000. The company will receive $1,200,000 for the shares from the warrant holders.

If the warrants were not exercised, and lapse unused, the effect is as if the company had received a gift. The special reserve for the warrants will be transferred to another reserve account in the balance sheet. In the example above, if the warrants were not exercised, when they lapse the $500,000 will be transferred from a balance-sheet reserve for the warrants to another equity reserve account, perhaps a general reserve account.

Accounting for Preferred Stock

Preferred stock is shown in the balance sheet of a company as share capital, but a clear distinction is made between equity share capital and reserves, and preferred stock capital that is non-equity share capital.

Accounting for the Redemption of Redeemable Shares

Preferred stock, as well as some convertible bonds, may be redeemed at a premium. Where there will be a premium on redemption, the company must make a finance charge each year, sufficient over the life of the shares or bonds to provide for the premium. The finance charge is not an equal amount every year. It is calculated at a constant rate of interest on the carrying amount of the shares or bonds in the company's balance sheet that rises as finance charges are provided for each year. The example below gives a simplified illustration.

Example

A company has issued 1,000,000 convertible redeemable 5% preferred stocks of $1 each. They are shown in the balance sheet at their par value, $1,000,000 and there are no finance charges for the issue. In practise, any finance costs incurred in making the share issue would be added to the carrying cost of the shares in the company's balance sheet. The shares are redeemable after five years at $1.20 per share. However, they also can be converted, any time from the end of year three, into equity shares of the company, at the rate of two ordinary shares of 25¢ each for each $1 preferred stock.

The company will begin by accounting for the stock as if they were to be redeemed rather than converted into equity shares. If they were redeemed, the cost of redemption, at $1.20 per share, would be $1,200,000. There is a finance charge of $200,000 to provide for. This will be done by making a finance charge each year against profits, and transferring this charge to a special redemption reserve account in the balance sheet.

Suppose the company calculates that the finance charges would be $36,000 in Year 1, $38,888 in Year 2, $40,000 in Year 3, $42,000 in Year 4 and $44,000 in Year 5.

The company would account for the preferred stock each year as follows, assuming the shares are not converted.

Year	**Carrying amount: start of year $000**	**Finance charge $000**	**Carrying amount: end of year $000**
1	1,000	36	1,036
2	1,036	38	1,074
3	1,074	40	1,114
4	1,114	42	1,156
5	1,156	44	1,200

Note: The carrying amount is the preferred stock capital of $1,000,000, plus the accumulated finance charges in the redemption reserve account in the balance sheet. By the end of year 5, there is a sufficient amount in the balance sheet to cover the redemption of the shares at the premium value. When the shares are redeemed for cash, the preferred stock capital of $1,000,000 and the redemption reserve account of $200,000 will disappear from the balance sheet of the company.

If the shares were converted into equity, the transaction would be recorded so that there would be no reported profit or loss on the transaction. In the example above, suppose that all the preferred stock is converted into equity shares at the end of year 3. The conversion would affect the balance sheet of the company as follows:

	Remove from balance sheet $	Add to balance sheet $
Preferred stock	$1,000,000	
Accumulated finance charges	$114,000	
Share capital (2,000,000 shares of 25¢)		$500,000
Reserves (share premium): the balance		$614,000
	$1,114,000	$1,114,000

Conclusion

The purpose of this book has been to describe hybrid instruments, their features and why they are used. This short chapter on accounting for hybrid instruments should help you to understand how companies report hybrid instruments in their annual report and accounts, and assist with the understanding and interpretation of corporate accounts.

Glossary

144A Market
US private placement market for unregistered securities.

Accrued Interest
Interest earned on a bond investment since the previous interest payment, and not yet paid to the bondholder.

Amps
Auction market preferred stock. A form of preferred stock for which the dividend is reset at regular auctions.

Black-Scholes Model
Mathematical model used as a basis for valuing options and warrants.

Bond Value
The market value a convertible bond would have if it were a straight fixed-rate bond with no conversion rights.

Book-Entry Transfer
Recording the transfer of ownership of a security by computer.

Breakeven/Payback
A ratio, expressed in years, that compares the size of a conversion premium with the difference between the yield on a convertible security and the dividend yield on the shares into which it can be converted. The concept of payback can be used to determine the appropriate size of a conversion premium.

Call Option
In the case of convertibles, the right of the issuer, but not an obligation, to redeem the securities before maturity at a stated price.

Clean Price
Market price of a bond, excluding accrued interest. The price at which bonds are traded in the markets.

Conduit Vehicles
See Special-Purpose Vehicles.

Covered Warrants
Share warrants issued by a dealer rather than by a company.

Conversion Premium
The amount by which a conversion price for a convertible bond exceeds the conversion value (current market value) of the shares into which it can be converted. Expressed as a percentage of the current market price for the share.

Conversion Price
The share price at which a convertible can be exchanged into shares on conversion. This sets the conversion ratio.

Conversion Ratio
Number of shares into which a convertible security can be converted. Usually derived from the conversion price.

Conversion Value
The current market value of the shares for which a convertible security can be exchanged on conversion. Also called Parity Value.

Coupon
The annual rate of interest payable on a bond, as a percentage of the bond's face value.

Credit Enhancement
Improving the credit rating of an issue of bonds by obtaining a third-party guarantee from a top-rated organization or credit-risk insurance.

Current Yield
Annual interest receivable from a security (bond or preferred stock) expressed as a percentage of its current market value. Also called interest yield.

Debt Warrant
Warrant entitling its holder to subscribe for a quantity of bonds at a fixed price.

Delayed Equity
A security or instrument, for example option or warrant, that can be converted into equity shares in the future.

Diminishing Bonds
An issue of bonds that is gradually being redeemed.

Dirty Price
Price payable for a bond on settlement of a purchase transaction. The dirty price consists of the clean price plus accrued interest.

Discount Paper
Short-term securities issued at a discount to face value and redeemed at par.

Equity Kicker
Term used to describe the attachment of share options or share warrants to an issue of bonds as a means of encouraging investors to subscribe for them.

Equity Warrant
See Share Warrant.

Equity Warrant Bond
Bond issued with share warrants attached.

Euroconvertibles
Convertible securities issued and traded on the international securities market (the euromarket).

Exchangeable Bond
A bond that can be exchanged, at the option of the bondholder or noteholder, into existing shares of another company, i.e. a company other than the company issuing the securities. The bond issuer should own the shares of the other company that it may need for exchanging the bonds when the bonds are first issued. In other respects, exchangeable bonds are similar to convertible bonds.

Exercise Period
Period during which an option or warrant can be exercised by its holder.

Exercise Price
The price at which an option or warrant can be exercised. It can be the price at which the option or warrant holder can subscribe for shares in the company, or the price at which a put option holder can have a bond redeemed (put price).

In-the-Money Warrants
Warrants for which the subscription price for equity shares is lower than the share's current market price.

International Primary Market Association (IPMA)
Self-regulatory organization for the primary (new issues) international securities markets.

International Securities Market Association (ISMA)
Self-regulatory organization of dealers in the secondary markets for international bonds.

Lead Manager
Investment bank or securities house that acts as main organizer for an issue of securities.

LIBOR

London Interbank Offered Rate. Interest rate at which highly rated banks will lend to each other in the money markets.

Mezzanine Finance

Finance that ranks below senior debt but above equity. A term used in the UK for part of the finance for a management buy-out (MBO) or management buy-in (MBI) consisting typically of bonds plus an equity kicker (options or warrants).

Mortgage-Backed Securities

Asset-backed securities where the underlying assets are mortgage loans.

Non-Equity Shares

Shares that are not equity. Principally preferred stock.

Out-of-the-Money Warrants

Warrants for which the subscription price for shares is above the share's current market price.

Parity Value

See Conversion Value.

Private Placement Market

US market for unregistered securities. Also called the 144A market.

Put Option

For convertibles, a right but not an obligation, of the holder to have the convertible redeemed before maturity at a fixed price, on a specified date or during a specified period.

Redemption Yield

The average annual return on a redeemable security, up to its redemption date, expressed as a percentage of the security's current market price.

Rolling Premium Put Convertibles

Convertible securities that give their holder a series of put options at different dates. The exercise price for the put option rises at each successive exercise date and is at a premium to par value.

Senior Debt
Secured debt that ranks ahead of other creditors in rights to payment, e.g. in the event of liquidation of the company.

Single-Premium Put Convertibles
Convertible securities that give their holder a put option. The redemption price for the put option is above (at a premium to) par value.

Special-Purpose Vehicle (SPV)
Company established for the purpose of issuing asset-backed securities. Also called conduit vehicle.

Yield to Put
The average annual return on a convertible security with a put option. It is expressed as a percentage of the security's current market price, on the assumption that the put option to redeem the security will be exercised at the next exercise date.

Zero-Coupon Convertibles
Convertible bonds issued at a discount to par and redeemable at a higher price, e.g. at par value at maturity, but on which no interest is paid. The investor earns a return from the profit between purchase price and redemption price.

Index